# EXODUS 34:19

## ALL THAT OPENETH THE MATRIX IS MINE...

Khary Ato Neblett

# Table of Contents

# PREFACE

When I was 17, I prayed in Jesus' name confessing that I was foolish and didn't want to act right. I asked The Lord to give me a sign to get my mind right when it's time so that I wouldn't die in sin or destroy myself. At the time I didn't fully understand the generational curses that were in my DNA. My grandfather on my mother's side was a gangster, and my father was a freedom fighter/SNCC freedom Singer in the 1960's human rights movement. My father told me that racism and injustice had him angry all of his life. The anger from my mother's side and my father's side manifested in me. I remember being scared of myself and what I might do when becoming angry.

My parents raised me in church, so as far as I can remember I had the fear of God. Around the age of 13, I beat my brother up for quitting a 1-on-1 basketball game that we were playing. He was mad because I was winning, and I was mad because he was emotional. He was acting like a punk and I didn't like it. That same night I went outside to pray. I asked God to help me deal with my anger. The Holy Spirit told me to smile before I react and think about how insignificant every situation is that can trigger my emotions. When I practiced being content regardless of the circumstances, I realized that demons operate through emotional people. Demons use offenses to make people destroy each other. Resentment and bitterness is a tool that destroys people from the inside out. We must forgive to be free. The same people that captured, lynched, and hung Jesus on a tree, Jesus forgave.

Luke 23:34 KJV "Then said Jesus, Father, forgive them; for they know not what they do. And they parted his raiment, and cast lots."

I went to University of Louisville with an academic scholarship but I wanted to be a gangster and make money selling drugs. At the age of 22 God answered my prayer and gave me a sign to get right so I wouldn't die in sin and destroy myself. I don't think it's possible for me to forget this testimony.

I remember it like it was yesterday. I was selling crack cocaine in my customers house and he had friends over so I was relaxing in a lazy boy chair watching the news by myself. The program began to show the wildfires in southern California, and that's when my mind began to think about how the book of Revelation says the earth will suffer from judgment, and Matthew 24 when Jesus said there will be wars and rumors of wars. As I was pondering on how September 11, 2001 triggered the Iraqi war on terror situation, the Holy Spirit came over me and said "Its Time." All I could do was hold my head in my hand, cry, and repeat the name Jesus over and over. The name of Jesus was keeping my mind focused and in agreement with receiving what God wanted me to know.

He told me that I was like my father in the sense that we are freedom fighters and soldiers for the children of God. My father is an activist. He risked his life in the 1960's human rights movement and never compromised for money, fame, or comfortability. My father was a foot soldier registering people to vote and SNCC Freedom Singer. He also led a protest at a Ku Klux Klan rally without a gun and only a few people were willing to come along. We don't have the spirit of fear. We love the truth and hate the lie. We lean towards wisdom, and debunk foolishness. We would rather be poor with a peace of mind knowing that we will never sell our soul, integrity, or purpose to be rich and forsake the revolutionary progression of the people.

God let me know that I have the gift of understanding so we can realize the Holy Spirit and the truth will make us free. Since childhood my father couldn't understand racism and he was mad all of his life. God showed me all the answers in the Bible for what racism is all about, and it just so happened that from two brown skin parents I was born white. God used the only white child out of four to be a prophet unto the nations to strengthen the faith of all those that are decieved by racism. God created racism and the devil doesn't want us to understand it so we can overcome. We shall overcome by the blood of The Lamb (Jesus Christ). God told me that he made me look like every nationality of people on the earth, so when I speak everyone will listen out of interest before casting judgment. I have African, European, Asian, and Native American characteristics so all people should be able to see themselves in me. When I pondered that revelation according to my purpose I began to learn some things that became a witnesses to who I am in Christ. Everyone has a purpose and most people will never know their true purpose until God reveals it to them.

The Lord told me that all of the precious metals and stones inside the earth are of Heaven. The precious metals and stones inside the earth are found in the soil. The soil is what God created man from, so the spiritual gifts that God gives us symbolize the precious metals and stones in the dirt we were created from. Anytime a person is driven to extract gold from the earth, there is work to be done. One may have to dig and shuffle dirt and mud in order to find it. Once the gold is extracted from the earth, it has to be cleaned, purified, or cut for it to shine. This means that everyone is born gifted, but we have to exercise our gifts and let God use our gifts by the cleansing of the Holy Spirit.

My purpose is to get you to use your brain, and teach you how to think according to spirit and truth. I'm not perfect, but I press towards the mark of the high calling. We don't wrestle against flesh and blood. Those that endure until the end will be saved. Saved from what? Eternal damnation in the Lake of Fire?

Matthew 17:9 says, "Every tree that bringeth forth not good fruit is hewn down and cast into the fire."

Revelation 12:11 says, "And they overcame him by the blood of the Lamb, and by the word of their testimony; and they loved not their lives unto the death."

There is symbolism in my genetics confirming my purpose. I didn't understand my purpose until it was revealed to me. I don't have pride in my calling. Only thing I have to boast about is God's mercy and grace. All knowledge, wisdom, and understanding comes from God. It's amazing how the Holy Ghost will truly lead you to all truth. God made me a messenger. I have no desire to be labeled a prophet, teacher, evangelist, preacher, apostle, or pastor. However, all I want to be is an obedient son of God. All I care about is giving God the glory and doing his will. I didn't ask for this. I was ordained for this.

Jesus said to seek and ye shall find, and he who hungers and thirst after righteousness shall be filled. The Lord put the desire to learn in my heart so his will can be done in my life for his name's sake. I've learned that everyone doesn't need Bible school to be in the ministry. We need to be called, have the Holy Spirit, know The Word, and have a relationship with God. We have to let that mind that be in Christ Jesus also be in us. How can we let that mind of Christ Jesus be in us if we don't know what Jesus Christ said.

Paul was used by Jesus because he was highly educated and could speak different languages. He could take the gospel to those of other nationalities and communicate the will of God effectively. He also had a determination and heart to fight for what he believed in. If Jesus wouldn't have given him that encounter on the road to Damascus, Paul wouldn't have known the mind of Christ for himself regardless of how educated he was. Having a relationship with God qualifies one for the ministry, not Seminary or Bible school.

The truth will make you free, and Jesus said "If you love me feed my sheep." Therefore I have to feed you the truth, so we all can be free. I have to be obedient to be free. Obedience is the key. Every walk is purpose driven to be married unto Jesus. As the 'Bride of Christ', we are called to keep his commandments. A disobedient wife is troubling to a husband and Jesus is the husbandman. The Lord has given me a gift of understanding and the spirit of knowledge. The word of God says, "If any man among you seem to become wise first let him become a a fool, that he may become wise." We all have to realize that we are born into sin, ignorance, pride, and our flesh is foolish. Until we can admit and confess the foolishness and iniquity within us we will never be wise. Life is about learning and God knows all things.

There are many things that you are going to learn if you listen with patience. How I opened the matrix, clearer understanding of the Bible, knowledge of God, why its power in the name of Jesus, who we are and why we are here, understanding the 12 tribes of Israel, the will of God for black and white people, and understanding Sex, drugs, and alcohol. I have documented all that the Lord has led me to write in one piece for the edification of the saints. As the saints are being edified, the unbeliever will have the choice of remaining foolish or taking heed to the cloud of witnesses provided that gives proof that the Bible is the true word of God. The Lord has given me the understanding of the prophecy, "The first shall be last and the last shall be first." This is impartation of an evolutionary understanding for this day and time, which was ordained to be revealed. It's not hidden, most people just can't see it. The will of God is for man to lose his pride, so that he will submit and be obedient. Every curse and movement by the hand of God was for a learning experience so that we can come to the ultimate understanding which is this: **Mankind has to lose pride, We wouldn't exist without God, without God we can do nothing, all creation has a purpose, the Holy Spirit is the only thing that can transform us into who we need to be, the Holy Spirit helps us to be obedient, let God be true and every man a liar, and it takes suffering for people to be thankful and to accept what God allows.**

**Romans 8:28-31** says, "And we know that all things work together for good to them that love God, to them who are the called according to his purpose." (Loving God is a willing act of man, but being called by God is an act of God. These are the only two groups of people on earth that have the capacity to give God glory. Therefore, God will work all things together for good so that this group of people have no excuse).

29. For whom he did foreknow, he also did predestinate to be conformed to the image of his Son, that he might be the firstborn among many brethren. The Lord knew us before the foundation of the world. Those people that lead us to Christ are born again people. Since they were born again, then they are the first born of all those they led to Christ.

30. Moreover whom he did predestinate, them he also called: and whom he called, them he also justified: and

whom he justified, them he also glorified. In order to fulfill his will, God can use anyone he wants to, and make the issues of life for a testimony work out in a person's favor to be profitable for the Gospel.

31. What shall we then say to these things? If God be for us, who can be against us?

**Daniel 12:4** says, "But thou, O Daniel, shut up the words, and seal the book, even to the time of the end: many shall run to and fro, and knowledge shall be increased." (There are vehicles that can get us from one side of the earth to another in hours when it used to take years. Now we can just google anything and get the Testimony `of Jesus Christ over the internet with no problem.)

**Ecclesiastes 3:14** says, "I know that, whatsoever God doeth, it shall be forever: nothing can be put to it, nor any thing taken from it: and God doeth it, that men should fear before him." God ordained slavery as a consequence of disobedience. He caused Israel to be obedient to their enemy in order to bring forth humility, the fear of the Lord, and obedience to that which profits. That which profits is the Holy Spirit.

**Mark 9:35** says, "And he sat down, and called the twelve, and saith unto them, If any man desire to be first, the same shall be last of all, and servant of all." We all have a desire to have things our way. Pride keeps us in a state unqualified for the Kingdom of Heaven. In order for us to be exalted by God we have to learn humility and servitude even if we have to endure servitude that is undesirable. By us understanding the trials of a servant, we can then understand what to consider as a leader.

**Matthew 20:16** says, "So the last shall be first, and the first last: for many be called, but few chosen."(Many people get put in a situation to be last so God can make them first, but only a few people past the test of servitude to be chosen to lead.)

- Lucifer was an angel exalted first in heaven – because of pride - Lucifer became last.
- Man was created lower than the angels, through salvation, we will be exalted higher than the angels and judge angels.
- Eve was created last, but was the first to sin.
- First man ruled over women, and in the last days women rule over man. Isaiah 3:12 says, "…and women rule over them."
- Adam was first, and Jesus was the second Adam. Adam caused death, and Jesus brings life.
- Abraham had Ishmael and Isaac. Ishmael was born first. Ishmael was born under the law. Isaac was born second. Isaac was born under the promise. Ishmael was born from logic or the law. Isaac was born from faith or grace.
- Esau was the first born and Jacob was the second born. Jacob got the birthright, and Esau became last.
- 2 Esdras 6:7-9 says, "Then answered I and said, What shall be the parting asunder of the times, or when shall be the end of the first, and the beginning of it that followeth?
- 8. And he said unto me, From Abraham unto Isaac, when Jacob and Esau were born of him, Jacob's hand held the heel of Esau.
- 9. For Esau is the end of the world, and Jacob is the beginning of it that followeth.
- Joseph was the last son out of all his brothers. Joseph was honored above all his brothers. Jacob clothed Joseph with a coat of many colors. The Father

clothed Jesus with a cloud and a rainbow of many colors in heaven. Read Revelation 4:3 and 10:1. Joseph saved the nation from the famine, and Jesus saves the world from hell. Joseph was sold into slavery because of his pride. He became high in the Kingdom, then was locked up and became low. Then he was released and became higher than all in the land. Jesus was first, made himself last, then he rose to be first again.

- Moses was found on the water escaping death as a child, then adopted by the Pharaoh. Moses became last banished from the land. Then Moses became first delivering the Israelites out of the Pharaoh's hands. Moses led the Israelites to the Promise Land, but for his pride Moses wasn't permitted to enter into the Promise land.
- Samson was the strongest man. Samson let a harlot make him last. Samson repented and God made him first again to kill all of his enemies with his last strength.
- David was the youngest son, with the worst job. God exalted David as King. David committed murder and adultery. David continuously repented, and had love for his enemies. David wasn't allowed to build God a temple for he had too much blood on his hands. David was a man after God's own heart, and God chose David's bloodline to be born into. The Tribe of Yahudah or Judah.
- Solomon was the wisest man on earth. Solomon let the foolish things (wicked women) turn his heart from God to serve other God's.
- The rich get their reward first on Earth. Jesus said, "Blessed are the poor in spirit: for theirs is the kingdom of heaven."
- Paul was last by blaspheming and persecuting the Jews (Judah). God made Paul first by making the

transition of the gospel to the gentiles for the last days, and he wrote most of the New Testament.

- The Jews (Israelites) had the Gospel first, then God gave the glory of the Gospel to the gentiles (Europeans) which were last.
- God was into the Hebrew heritage, which was first. (Had a Hebrew name Yahshua). Then took on the Gentile heritage which was last. (Name went to Jesus)
- The black man was first, and the white man was last. Then God made the white man first, and the black man last.
- White men was separated from the black man at first. Then the black man was separated from the white man at last.
- The black man killed many white men at first. Then the white man killed many more black men at last.
- African Americans are Hebrew Israelites. The Knights Templar (army of the Roman Empire) ran the Israelites into Africa when they raided Jerusalem. The Israelites migrated from one African Nation to another and many ended up in West Africa. West Africa is where the Atlantic slave trade occurred. The Ishmaelites/Muslims were in Africa killing and enslaving the black Jews (Judah)since they were concidered disposable fugitives. The Muslims and Africans had the Hebrews as servants (working class), so they traded them on to the Europeans for guns. Slavery made the Israelites last among all nations. Now the whole world wants to be a part of the culture the Israelites have created. Michael Jordan, Serena Williams, Michael Jackson, Dr. King etc… are all Hebrews.
- Prophets are persecuted and last as servavnts on earth, but obtain the greatest gift and will have treasure in heaven.

- Jeremiah 25:4 says, And the LORD hath sent unto you all his servants the prophets, rising early and sending them, but ye have not hearkened, nor inclined your ear to hear.
- The sign of speaking in tongues was first at the day of Pentacost. The sign of prophecy is the last sign concerning the last days.
- Acts 2:17 says, "And it shall come to pass in the last days, saith God, I will pour out of my Spirit upon all flesh: and your sons and your daughters shall prophesy, and your young men shall see visions, and your old men shall dream dreams."
- 1 Corinthians 14:1 says, "Follow after charity, and desire spiritual gifts, but rather that ye may prophesy.
- 2. For he that speaketh in an unknown tongue speaketh not unto men, but unto God: for no man understandeth him; howbeit in the spirit he speaketh mysteries.
- 3. But he that prophesieth speaketh unto men to edification, and exhortation, and comfort.
- 4. He that speaketh in an unknown tongue edifieth himself; but he that prophesieth edifieth the church.
- 5. I would that ye all spake with tongues, but rather that ye prophesied: for greater is he that prophesieth than he that speaketh with tongues, except he interpret, that the church may receive edifying."
- Slavery in Egypt was the first house of bondage. Slavery in America is the last house of bondage.
- The Promise land was the first Jerusalem. New Jerusalem is the last Promise Land.

# INTRODUCTION

My name 'Khary' means **'He who walks with God.'** My middle name 'Ato' means **'Brilliant.' Proverbs 22** says **"A good name is rather to be chosen than great riches, and loving favour rather than silver and gold.**

**Ephesians 4:11** says, "And he gave some, apostles; and some, prophets; and some, evangelists; and some, pastors and teachers; for the perfecting of the saints, for the work of the ministry, for the edifying of the body of Christ.

**Jeremiah 1:5** says, "Before I formed thee in the belly I knew thee; and before you came forth out of the womb I sanctified thee, and I ordained thee a prophet unto the nations."

**Deuteronomy 18:18** says, "I will raise them up a Prophet from among their brethren, like unto thee, and will put my words in his mouth; and he shall speak unto them all that I shall command him."

**1 Corinthians 14:37-39** says, "If any man think himself to be a prophet, or spiritual, let him acknowledge that the things that I write unto you are the commandments of the Lord. But if any man be ignorant, let him be ignorant. Wherefore, brethren, covet to prophesy, and forbid not to speak with tongues."

**1 Corinthians 13:2** says, "And though I have the gift of prophecy, and understand all mysteries, and all knowledge; and though I have all faith, so that I could remove mountains, and have not charity, I am nothing.

**Matthew 11:25** says, "At that time Jesus answered and said, "I thank thee, O Father, Lord of heaven and earth, because thou hast hid these things from the wise and prudent, and hast revealed them unto babes."

**1 Corinthians 1:27** says, "But God hath chosen the foolish things of the world to confound the wise; and God hath chosen the weak things of the world to confound the things which are mighty."

**1 Corinthians 2:5** says, "That your faith should not stand in the wisdom of men, but in the power of God."

**Ecclesiastes 3:11** says, "He hath made every thing beautiful in his time: also he hath set the world in their heart, so that no man can find out the work that God maketh from the beginning to the end."

*****1 Corinthians 3:18** says, **"Let no man deceive himself. If any man among you seemeth to be wise in this world, let him become a fool, that he may be wise."*****

# First Born Sons Open the Matrix

## Jesus Christ is the Matrix

## (First Born Son)

**Exodus 34:19** says, "**All that openeth the matrix is mine**; and every firstling among thy cattle, whether ox or sheep, that is male."

**Exodus 13:12** says, "**That thou shalt set apart unto the LORD all that openeth the matrix**, and every firstling that cometh of a beast which thou hast; the males shall be the LORD'S."

**Numbers 3:12** says, "And I, behold, **I have taken the Levites from among the children of Israel instead of all the firstborn that openeth the matrix among the children of Israel**: therefore the Levites shall be mine."

**Numbers 18:15** says, "**Every thing that openeth the matrix in all flesh, which they bring unto the LORD, whether it be of men or beasts, shall be thine**: nevertheless the firstborn of man shalt thou surely redeem, and the firstling of unclean beasts shalt thou redeem."

**Exodus 13:15** says, "And it came to pass, when Pharaoh would hardly let us go, that the LORD slew all the firstborn in the land of Egypt, both the firstborn of man, and the firstborn of beast: **therefore I sacrifice to the LORD all that openeth the matrix, being males; but all the firstborn of my children I redeem**."

*** Ephesians 3:9 says, "And to make all men see what is the fellowship of the mystery, which from the**

**beginning of the world hath been hid in God, who created all things by Jesus Christ."** *

The matrix of Jesus Christ concerning order is a pyramid with the godhead at the top. All of the first born sons of Israel (Levite priesthood) is under the godhead. The rest of Israel is under the priesthood. The other nations are under Israel, and Edom is on the bottom.

**Obadiah 1:1-4** says, "The vision of Obadiah. Thus saith the Lord GOD concerning Edom; We have heard a rumour from the LORD, and an ambassador is sent among the heathen, Arise ye, and let us rise up against her in battle.

2. Behold, I have made thee small among the heathen: thou art greatly despised.

3. The pride of thine heart hath deceived thee, thou that dwellest in the clefts of the rock, whose habitation is high; that saith in his heart, Who shall bring me down to the ground?

4. Though thou exalt thyself as the eagle, and though thou set thy nest among the stars, thence will I bring thee down, saith the LORD."

The matrix of Satan according to his structure is himself at the top of the pyramid. The fallen angels under him. The evil spirits are under the fallen angels. Edomites with fallen angel DNA are under the evil spirits. Edomites that are human, under satanic oaths, are under the genetically modified Edomites. The other nations come next, and Israel is on the bottom.

Babylon, Persia, Greece, and Rome are the four kingdoms that would rise and fall in Daniel chapter two.

Each one of these kingdoms had a ruling monarch with fallen angel DNA. The right to rule came by bloodline. Babylon and Persia were black people. Greece and Rome are white people. Israel was captive in all four of these kingdoms. Regardless of the nation of Israel's captivity, God chose Israel to be the light in the darkness. Stated in Daniel 2:43, Rome (Edom) is the last kingdom that will try to mingle the iron (mark of the beast technology) with the miry clay (humans).

Daniel 2:43-44 says, "And whereas thou sawest iron mixed with miry clay, they shall mingle themselves with the seed of men: but they shall not cleave one to another, even as iron is not mixed with clay.

44. And in the days of these kings shall the God of heaven set up a kingdom, which shall never be destroyed: and the kingdom shall not be left to other people, but it shall break in pieces and consume all these kingdoms, and it shall stand for ever."

**Jesus is the first born of creation. Jesus inheritance comes from the Father, and his inheritance is the souls of those that are saved by grace through faith. The bride of Christ and the body of Christ are the chosen.** First born sons of the faith are to be an example to lead the way for everyone else. Jesus endured till the end, and those that endure till the end will be saved. Jesus lived a life of fasting and prayer. Jesus showed us how to walk in the Holy Spirit and deny the flesh. Sin is condemed in the flesh. The dietary laws and medicines of the earth are for the pineal gland (heart) of man to connect to the spirit of God without static, and for man to simply operate in full compacity.

**The law shows man what sin is, and why punishment is important so sin doesn't spread like wildfire. Some sin was punishable by death, because felony sins attract powerful demons.** Once demonic principalities set up in a region, it is hard to break their stronghold when sin is the lifestyle of the people. People are 'monkey see monkey do.' God has to show chosen people what the majority of people cannont see. Since we evolve into what we see and hear, prophets are neccessary to proclaim truth so people will have a voice of truth/reasoning in a dark world of lies. **Satan doesn't create, he only perverts what God created.**

**Deuteronomy 22:22** says, "If a man be found lying with a woman married to an husband, then they shall both of them die, both the man that lay with the woman, and the woman: so shalt thou put away evil from Israel."

**Leviticus 20:13** says, "If a man also lie with mankind, as he lieth with a woman, both of them have committed an abomination: they shall surely be put to death; their blood shall be upon them."

Jesus showed us that the weapons of our warfare are not carnal. We fight in prayer and fasting. Nothing good comes without sacrifice, but obedience is better than sacrifice. It is better to stay sin free than to continue in sacrifice for sin. Once we recieve the blood of Jesus (red pill), then our mission is to war with the demonic strongholds that came from sin (generational curses). We recieve angels to protect us from demons, and they also minister to us keeping us edifyed. We fortify our life by the words we speak and how we believe. We stay demon free when we are sin free. Sin is fun for a season, but when we began to reap what we have sown, we must remember to take heed to correction and repent daily.

**Hebrews 11:24** says, "By faith Moses, when he was come to years, refused to be called the son of Pharaoh's daughter;

**25. Choosing rather to suffer affliction with the people of God, than to enjoy the pleasures of sin for a season;**

26. Esteeming the reproach of Christ greater riches than the treasures in Egypt: for he had respect unto the recompence of the reward.

27. By faith he forsook Egypt, not fearing the wrath of the king: for he endured, as seeing him who is invisible.

**28. Through faith he kept the passover, and the sprinkling of blood, lest he that destroyed the firstborn should touch them.**

**Matthew 16:19** says, "And I will give unto thee the keys of the kingdom of heaven: and whatsoever thou shalt bind on earth shall be bound in heaven: and whatsoever thou shalt loose on earth shall be loosed in heaven."

**Jesus is the first born of all people on earth. The matrix is Jesus Christ because the world was created according to the fullness of Jesus and what he represents from his head to his feet.** The Father has no beginning. Jesus is the beginning and the end. . Beginning and end are opposites. Jesus and Lucifer are opposites. Humility and pride are opposites. Obedience and disobedience are opposites. Blessings and curses are opposites. Good and evil are opposites. Sun and moon are opposites. The earth and sky (heavens) are opposites. Man and woman are opposites. Black and white are opposites.

**The matrix of Jesus Christ shows us that we need his blood (red pill) for the Holy Spirit for man cannot earn salvation on his own merit.**

**Ecclesiastes 3:11** says, "He hath made every thing beautiful in his time: also he hath set the world in their heart, so that no man can find out the work that God maketh from the beginning to the end."

**Genesis 6:6** says, "And it repented the LORD that he had made man on the earth, and it grieved him at his heart."

**Hebrews 9:22** says, "And almost all things are by the law purged with blood; and without shedding of blood is no remission."

**James 2:10** says, "For whosoever shall keep the whole law, and yet offend in one point, he is guilty of all."

**Matthew 15:24** says, "But he answered and said, I am not sent but unto the lost sheep of the house of Israel."

**Ephesians 2:8** says, "For by grace are ye saved through faith; and that not of yourselves: it is the gift of God.
9. Not of works, lest any man should boast."

**Acts 2:17** says, "And it shall come to pass in the last days, saith God, I will pour out of my Spirit upon all flesh: and your sons and your daughters shall prophesy, and your young men shall see visions, and your old men shall dream dreams."

**Romans 8:16** says, "The Spirit itself beareth witness with our spirit, that we are the children of God."

**Revelation 20:4** says, "**And I saw thrones, and they sat upon them, and judgment was given unto them: and I saw the souls of them that were beheaded for the witness of Jesus, and for the word of God, and which had not worshipped the beast, neither his image, neither had received his mark upon their foreheads, or in their hands; and they lived and reigned with Christ a thousand years."**

**5. But the rest of the dead lived not again until the thousand years were finished. This is the first resurrection."**

**2 Esdras 13:22-24** says, "**Whereas thou hast spoken of them that are left behind, this is the interpretation:**

**23. He that shall endure the peril in that time hath kept himself: they that be fallen into danger are such as have works, and faith toward the Almighty.**

**24. Know this therefore, that they which be left behind are more blesssed than they that be dead."**

**The opposite of the six days of the week is the Sabbath day.** Six days man is to work, but on the Sabbath day man is to rest and keep it holy. The opposite of work is to rest and recharge spiritually in order to keep working. Fasting, praying, and cleansing the body is ideal for the Sabbath day. The earth can only exist within the time frame God allows which is 7 days. The seventh day or last thousand years, is the last day which is the opposite of the past six days/six thousand years. Those that are masters at the end of the world will be servants at the beginning of the world that comes after. The world that comes after is the Sabbath day and a day unto the Lord is one thousand years.

**Those that will reign one thousand years are in correllation with the Joshuah generation that took the promise land and didn't have a slave mentality.**

**The earth was created in 6 days and God rested on the 7th day or Sabbath day.** God put in work for 6 days and rested on the 7th day. Work and resting are opposites. God ordained the return of Jesus Christ to be at the end of 6,000 years, which is 6 days, because 1,000 years is one day to God. The last thousand years, which is the sabbath day, Jesus will bring down New Jerusalem from heaven. Their will be peace on earth, and we will enter into God's rest. Resting is the opposite of oppression, despair, and slave labor.

**The 12 Tribes of Israel are God's chosen people by the way of the faithful, Shemite, Caldean, or the Hebrew 'Abraham'.** By their pride, Israel was disobedient just like God figured they would be, so he allowed them to go into slavery. Since the children of Israel didn't wan't to be humble and obey God, he put them into the hands of their enemies for them to see how Satan will treat them. The will of God is for Israel to repent and turn back to God, because people are 'monkey see monkey do.' Israel has the most influence on earth even in poverty. God made Edom/Esau the first born of Isaac, and Ishmael the first born of Abraham. Edom/Esau would rule the world at the end of the 6 days. Edom enslaved Israel in Greece, Rome, and the Americas. Ishmaelites enslaved Israelites in Africa. This is why it was easy for Ishmaelites to hand over the captivity of Israel, which is Jacob in Africa, into the hands of Edom. Edom created Christianity, and Ishmaelites created Islam.

**Amos 1:6** says, "Thus saith the LORD; For three transgressions of Gaza, and for four, I will not turn away the punishment thereof; because they carried away captive the whole captivity, to deliver them up to Edom."

**Amos 1:9** says, "Thus saith the LORD; For three transgressions of Tyrus, and for four, I will not turn away the punishment thereof; because they delivered up the whole captivity to Edom, and remembered not the brotherly covenant."

**Amos 1:11** says, "Thus saith the LORD; For three transgressions of Edom, and for four, I will not turn away the punishment thereof; because he did pursue his brother with the sword, and did cast off all pity, and his anger did tear perpetually, and he kept his wrath for ever."

**Israel went into 7 major captivities as follows: Babylon, Assyria, Persia, Greece, Rome, Egypt (Africa), and the Americas.** Seven is the number of completion. The 7th day, or the 7,000th year is the day of rest for the remnant of the 12 Tribes of Israel. All other nations of people who refuse to take the mark of the beast will be allowed to reign, but will be in servitude to Israel. No worries, for Israel having the structure of Jesus Christ (the matrix) as leadership will show all nations how God intended the world to operate in the beginning. **The 1,000 years of rest for Israel is the opposite of the slavery Israel endured within the 6,000 years or six days.**

**Amos 9:12-15** says, "That they may possess the remnant of Edom, and of all the heathen, which are called by my name, saith the LORD that doeth this.

13. Behold, the days come, saith the LORD, that the plowman shall overtake the reaper, and the treader of grapes him that soweth seed; and the mountains shall drop sweet wine, and all the hills shall melt.

14. And I will bring again the captivity of my people of Israel, and they shall build the waste cities, and inhabit them; and they shall plant vineyards, and drink the wine thereof; they shall also make gardens, and eat the fruit of them.

15. And I will plant them upon their land, and they shall no more be pulled up out of their land which I have given them, saith the LORD thy God."

**Revelation 21:1-4** says, "And I saw a new heaven and a new earth: for the first heaven and the first earth were passed away; and there was no more sea.

2. And I John saw the holy city, new Jerusalem, coming down from God out of heaven, prepared as a bride adorned for her husband.

3. And I heard a great voice out of heaven saying, Behold, the tabernacle of God is with men, and he will dwell with them, and they shall be his people, and God himself shall be with them, and be their God.

4. And God shall wipe away all tears from their eyes; and there shall be no more death, neither sorrow, nor crying, neither shall there be any more pain: for the former things arc passed away.

**Revelation 21:10-12** says, "And he carried me away in the spirit to a great and high mountain, and shewed me that great city, the holy Jerusalem, descending out of heaven from God,

11. Having the glory of God: and her light was like unto a stone most precious, even like a jasper stone, clear as crystal;

12. And had a wall great and high, and had twelve gates, and at the gates twelve angels, and names written thereon, which are the names of the twelve tribes of the children of Israel."

**Revelation 21:23-27** say, "And the city had no need of the sun, neither of the moon, to shine in it: for the glory of God did lighten it, and the Lamb is the light thereof.

24. And the nations of them which are saved shall walk in the light of it: and the kings of the earth do bring their glory and honour into it.

25. And the gates of it shall not be shut at all by day: for there shall be no night there.

26. And they shall bring the glory and honour of the nations into it.

27. And there shall in no wise enter into it any thing that defileth, neither whatsoever worketh abomination, or maketh a lie: but they which are written in the Lamb's book of life."

## Jacob And Esau Show Us

## Opposites Within The Matrix

**2 Esdras 6:9** says, "For Esau is the end of the world, and Jacob is the beginning of it that followeth. **(Esau is ruling the world at the end of the world, and Jacob will rule over the world to come at its beginning). The world that followeth is the 1000 year reign with the lion of Judah (Yahudah). After the 1000 years expire is the final judgement.**

**Genesis 25:23** says, "And the LORD said unto her, **Two nations** are in thy womb, and **two manner of people** shall be separated from thy bowels; **and the one people shall be stronger than the other people; and the elder shall serve the younger**."

24. And when her days to be delivered were fulfilled, behold, there were **twins in her womb.**

**25. And the first came out red, all over like an hairy garment; and they called his name Esau.**

Esau was a red head hairy albino (neanderthal), which was the opposite of Jacob. Esau ate bloody meat which was forbidden by God's law. Esau was deceitful and a killer, for he was always hunting animals. Esau didn't have honor for the heritage of his parents. Esau didn't care about his seed, much of his wives had fallen angel DNA, and some of his daughters were given to men of the same.

**Jasher 28:19-20** says, "And Esau was continually hunting in the fields to bring home what he could get, so did Esau all the days.

20. And Esau was a designing and deceitful man, one who hunted after the hearts of men and inveigled them, and Esau was a valiant man in the field, and in the course of time went as usual to hunt; and he came as far as the field of Seir, the same is Edom."

**Genesis 25:30** says, "And Esau said to Jacob, Feed me, I pray thee, with that same **red pottage**; for I am faint: therefore was his name called Edom." **(Red Pottage was bloody meat)**

**Jasher 30:28** says, "But from time to time Esau would go and see his father and mother in the land of Canaan, and **Esau intermarried with the Horites, and he gave his daughters to the sons of Seir, the Horite.**

**Jasher 29:14-16** says, "**And the wives of Esau vexed and provoked Isaac and Rebecca with their works, for they walked not in the ways of the Lord, but served their father's gods of wood and stone as their father had taught them, and they were more wicked than their father.**

15. And they went according to the evil desires of their hearts, and they sacrificed and burnt incense to the Baalim, and Isaac and Rebecca became weary of them.

16. And Rebecca said, I am weary of my life because of the daughters of Heth; if Jacob take a wife of the daughters of Heth, such as these which are of the daughters of the land, what good then is life unto me?"

Jacob didn't care about hunting and killing, for he took care of the garden and what came from the earth. Jacob was a trickster. However he obtained the birthright and blessing, it was for the will of God by the promise of God. God showed Jacob that everyone has to reap what they sow. God showed Jacob that nothing good comes without sacrifice. God showed Jacob that the blessing comes with a cost. Must lose the pride and be humble before the omnipresent spirit of God.

Jacob was decieved and manipulated by his uncle. Jacob took advantage of his blessing of abundance and left his uncle without giving him a chance to kiss his children; for Jacob was afraid that he would be manipulated again. Jacob had to wrestle with an angel before he recieved deliverance from the destruction of his brother Esau. The injury Jacob recieved was to remind him that his humility saved his life. Jacob recieved a physical thorn in the flesh to keep him humble. Jacob's humility and determination to be blessed saved him from the destruction of Esau.

Now, Esau is at the end of the world and Jacob (Israel) is in trouble. We have to come out from among the world and be set apart to be safe from manipulation/deception. We all have to do what Jacob did and cry out to God. Our disfunction is our thorn in the flesh. God showed Jacob that our purpose is to wrestle with God and man. Although people can be difficult to deal with, we still have to feed the sheep. We have to bless, love, and forgive people for God to forgive us. We have to hold on to God until he blesses us and never let him go.

**Jasher 31:65** says, "And Esau hastened and took his children and servants and the souls of his household, being sixty men, and he went and assembled all the children of Seir the Horite and their people, being three hundred and forty men, and took all this number of four hundred men with drawn swords, and he went unto Jacob to smite him."

**Jasher 32:27** says, "**And the Lord heard the prayer of Jacob on that day, and the Lord then delivered Jacob from the hands of his brother Esau.**"

**Genesis 32:25** says, "And when he saw that he prevailed not against him, he touched the hollow of his thigh; and the hollow of Jacob's thigh was out of joint, as he wrestled with him."

**2 Corinthians 12:7** says, "And lest I should be exalted above measure through the abundance of the revelations, there was given to me a thorn in the flesh, the messenger of Satan to buffet me, lest I should be exalted above measure."

**Philippians 2:12** says, "Wherefore, my beloved, as ye have always obeyed, not as in my presence only, but now much more in my absence, **work out your own salvation with fear and trembling."**

**1 Thessalonians 5:17** says, "**Pray without ceasing**."

Black, white, blue and red are the main colors of the matrix. Black and white symbolize each end of the color spectrum (beginning and end). Everything exist in between white and black. White and black people have red blood, and the blood of Jesus is what white and black people need to be saved from the red flames of the lake of fire. Blood is blue before comming in contact with oxygen. Fire has a blue flame, and white people can have blue eyes. The Black man was created from black soil which is the richest soil in a garden. The woman and the white man was created from the black man. The woman was created from the rib of the black man, and the white man was created from the black man by the predestination of God to illustrate a physical representation of pride. Pride is the first sin that leads to disobedience. Disobedience will lead to disorder. God is order. It's our Father's way and no disorder allowed.

The woman and the white man show the black man the levels of pride that exist inside of the black man. The woman symbolize the color red because Eve brought pride and disobedience. The disobedience resulted in sin and there is no forgiveness of sin without an accepted blood sacrifice. The woman bleeds every month because she got the bleeding started. The woman's actions lead to death, but the woman has a matrix (womb) to incubate life on earth.

The white man brings forth humility and correction to the black man by showing the world what pride looks like in physical form. All pride comes with a fall, and falls hurt. of white people turn red from heat. Painful correction is the only way God can bring his people to repent and stay humble. Prophecy persuades belief when nothing else will. Without conviction there is no repentance. Red blood cells car oxygen (spirit) to the cells. White blood cells (white people) deal with infections which symbolizes a reaction that brings healing and correction. What the devil meant for evil, God meant the white man for good. This is why the woman and the white man is ruling over the black man at the end of this age as a recompense for disobedience.

**Ecclesiastes 7:13** says, "Consider the work of God: for who can make that straight, which he hath made crooked?"

**Isaiah 1:18** says, "Come now, and let us reason together, saith the LORD: though your sins be as scarlet, they shall be as white as snow; though they be red like crimson, they shall be as wool."

Black and darkness are opposites. Black is the fullness of color, and darkness is the absence of color. White and light are opposites. White is the absence of color, and light is the fullness of color. When all the colors are mixed together you get black, but no color exist in darkness.

The description of Jesus deals with his head and feet. Head and feet are opposites. The head carries us in the spiritual, but our feet carry us physicaly. The head of Jesus symbolize the sky and imagery of albinos. The head of Jesus is described as white like wool and eyes as a flame of fire. The clouds are white like wool, the sky is blue, and the sun symbolizes a flame of fire. Albinos born from black people have hair white like wool, and can have eyes that are red, orange, yellow, green, blue (sky), indigo, and/or violet; which are the colors of the rainbow. White people evolved form albinos. Fire has a blue and a red flame along with the other colors flames can have depending on the material that is ignited. Since the sky is blue, most white people have blue eyes.

The feet of Jesus is as brass (brown) as if they burned in a furnace (black). Every metal that burns turn black on the outside and red on the inside, which correlates to his eyes as a flame of fire. We have fire inside the earth (magma) and fire in the sky (sun). Black people correlate to the feet of Jesus (black and brown), but all of our blood is blue and red like fire (blue flame and red flame). Black people come from the two sons of Noah, Shem and Ham. White people come from the son of Noah 'Japheth', and the son of Isaac 'Esau'. Jacob and Esau were twins, so Esau was albino and Jacob was black. Noah was albino and he had two black sons and one son (Japheth) that inherited the albino gene. Abraham came form the bloodline of Shem. Shem was black. Ham was black. Japheth's bloodline evolved into the white people we know today. The white people that have a genetic predisposition to hate black people mostly come from the bloodline of Esau (Edomites).

**Genesis 10:2-5** says, "The sons of Japheth; Gomer, and Magog, and Madai, and Javan, and Tubal, and Meshech, and Tiras. 3And the sons of Gomer; **Ashkenaz (an Ashkenazi Jew is a contradiction)**, and Riphath, and Togarmah.

4. And the sons of Javan; Elishah, and Tarshish, Kittim, and Dodanim.

5. By these were the isles of the **Gentiles** divided in their lands; every one after his tongue, after their families, in their nations." **(Gentiles are white people)**

The clouds are white like wool, and the flame of fire is the sun. The sun is all by itself as the eye in the sky, and the pineal gland is by itself as our third eye. The eye (pineal gland) is the organ we connect to the spirit with. It is energized by spirit which is electricity. Our heart pumps by the electricity that comes from the pineal gland. The heart in our chest is our physical heart, and the pineal gland (third eye) in our brain is our spiritual heart.

The eye inside of the earth is the inner core. The inner core is electricity powered by God. Lightening actually comes from the inner core inside the earth. Thunder and Lightening symbolize the voice of God which is the true light in the darkness. Lightening can light up the night sky more so than the moon. Thunder and lightening is a reminder that the wrath of God is terrible against darkness. Jesus Christ is the light in the darkness. This world is decieved by moon light (Satan). **Thunder and lightning says, "Fear God and keep his commandments so I can open up the windows of heaven and pour you out a blessing."**

We either conect to the holy spirit or an evil spirit. The sun symbolizes Jesus Christ. Jesus is by himself giving us the only source of life which is the holy spirit. The moon symbolizes Lucifer/Satan and the stars symbolize the fallen angels/demons. The moon looks like light, but its not real light because nothing can grow and live under moonlight alone. Jesus is represented by the day, and Satan's kingdom is represented by the night. This is why bats and owls come out at night. Jesus has day animals like eagles and butterflies which get their energy from the sun. All nocturnal animals hunt other animals and scavenge. Most day animals eat from the earth and make themselves useful for man.

**Revelation 1:14-15** says, "His head and his hairs were white like wool, as white as snow; and his eyes were as a flame of fire; **(Albino characteristics are in the sky - red, white and blue)**

15. And his feet like unto fine brass, as if they burned in a furnace; and his voice as the sound of many waters.**(Melenated men's characteristics are in the soil - black and brown).**

**Matthew 5:36** says, "Neither shalt thou swear by thy head, because thou canst not make one hair white or black." **(The older a person, the more their hair color reflects the white clouds or hair of Jesus Christ).**

The matrix is an environment or material in which something develops; a surrounding medium or structure, or a mass of fine-grained rock in which gems, crystals, or fossils are embedded. God created the matrix we live in. God created the environment and all the materials or resources that we need to develop. The mass of fine-grained rock in which gems, crystals, or fossils are embedded can relate to the revelation God gave me about spiritual gifts in people which correlate with the precious stones in heaven and the precious stones in the earth that man was created from. DNA is of crystal.

**Revelation 4:3** says, "And he that sat was to look upon like a jasper and a sardine stone: and there was a rainbow round about the throne, in sight like unto an emerald."

Satan knows about all the activities, games, sports, events, dinners, vehicles and technology God has in heaven. Satan has to create some of the things which are in heaven, on earth, to persuade men to sell their soul for pleasure and convenience. God can give a person instruction to build or create something, because it is in the bounds of what is already in heaven. Satan can give people knowledge of technology, but he needs the resources that God placed on earth. Man has dominion in the earth, so Satan has to use man to do the work for him. People that work for Satan are decieved by the love of money, power, and materialistic things he has to offer. Heaven has more than this earth could ever have, and people sell their souls for the things Satan presents to them on earth. Satan knows that his plan to kill, steal, and destroy has to come by technology. Many Africans are in slavery by minning all the resources Satan needs for technology. All of the earth's resources are used for various technology, artificial inteligence, and the hadron collider at Cern, Switzerland.

The matrix is the world we live in subjected to the limitations of Jesus Christ. The womb of the woman that allows a fetus to develop is a matrix that correllates to the matrix. The nourishment of a woman's womb correlates to being 'born again' of the water, Spirit, and blood that poored out of Jesus. When a woman's water breaks, blood is also present as the child comes forth. When the child comes forth, it has to take the breath of life to continue living.

Moreover, the matrix is subject to God's laws, statutes, and commandments within his construct that is designed for his will to be done on earth as it is in heaven. The man has dominion, and men are responsible for making sure God's standard is upheld. The laws and commandments of God keep order. Obedience to God provides safety and protection. Disobedience to God, by law, results in the lack of protection that allows demonic principalities to kill, steal, and destroy in several ways.

God gave his laws, statutes, and commandment to only one nation of people, and that nation is Israel. Israel was ordained by God to be an example to other nations as the light of the world, the salt of the earth, a peculiar people, and a royal priesthood. The Levites were the priesthood of Israel that were set apart to uphold the tabernacle in holiness, and make atonement for the people. When God killed the firstborn son of all the Egyptians along with those who didn't apply the blood on their door post, God wanted Israel to give him all of the first born males of all of their cattle. The first born sons were to be redeemed by the sacrifice of a lamb, goat, or cow because they are the cleanest animals. God didn't want Israel to sacrifice their children phsically, but to sacrifice the firstborn of the purest animals instead.

God was setting up the understanding that the first born son of the children of Israel is crucial to the development of the entire nation, therefore the first born son is to be educated in holiness. The first born son has to be the leader for those that come after him. God took the Levites for himself so they would not recieve inheritance on earth, but in heaven. The tithe of food were for the Levite priesthood so they could serve God to the fullest without spending so much time doing physical labor, for their time would be spent in spiritual labor. The Levites were ordained to keep the nation of Israel in order. The Levites symbolize the first born sons.

When God brought Israel out of the land of Egypt, he had to build up their belief in him because he knew they would return to Egypt for uncertainty. God wanted to lead Israel through the land of the Philistines, but he knew they would be afraid if they saw war. Fear and unbelief was such a stronghold on the minds of the people that God gave them a holiday called 'The feast of Unleavened Bread'/'The Passover' for them to observe every year and remember how he delivered them out of Egypt.

Unleavened bread symbolizes holiness without sin, and the law of God shows us what sin is. The small foxes destroy the vine, and a little leaven leaveneth the whole lump. Unleavened bread is pure grain without yeast. It doesn't rise so its thick, flat and dark. White bread is made from white flour, and white flour is made by a process that removes the bran, germ, fiber, vitamins and minerals leaving only the endosperm. White bread is the opposite of unleavened bread. God gave us dietary laws to keep us in good health, but look at us now as we suffer from so many health issues. Who told you tha bacon, sausage and pancakes was breakfast food? Fruit and herbs are breakfast food, because that is what we are suppose to break the fast with. This is why many sins were punishable by death because when sin is left uncorrected, it will spread like wildfire.

The Passover is significant for the blood of a lamb (sheep or goat) on the doorpost for the death angel to pass by. The blood of a sheep or goat is the symbolism of the blood of Jesus Christ. Jesus Christ is the lamb of God. The blood of Jesus Christ is the only recompense for sin. The blood of animals was a place holder for the blood of Jesus Christ. Jesus descended into Abraham's bosom, after he died, to retrieved all the souls that were covered by the blood of animals to redeemed them through the blood of Christ. The blood of Jesus is the only way any man can have his sins forgiven.

**Luke 22:1** says, "Now the feast of unleavened bread drew nigh, which is called the Passover."

**Exodus 12:5** says, "**Your lamb shall be without blemish, a male of the first year: ye shall take it out from the sheep, or from the goats:**

6. And ye shall keep it up until the fourteenth day of the same month: and the whole assembly of the congregation of Israel shall kill it in the evening.

7. And they shall take of the blood, and strike it on the two side posts and on the upper door post of the houses, wherein they shall eat it.

8. And they shall eat the flesh in that night, roast with fire, and unleavened bread; and with bitter herbs they shall eat it.

9. Eat not of it raw, nor sodden at all with water, but roast with fire; his head with his legs, and with the purtenance thereof.

10. And ye shall let nothing of it remain until the morning; and that which remaineth of it until the morning ye shall burn with fire.

11. And thus shall ye eat it; with your loins girded, your shoes on your feet, and your staff in your hand; and ye shall eat it in haste: it is the LORD'S passover.

**12. For I will pass through the land of Egypt this night, and will smite all the firstborn in the land of Egypt, both man and beast; and against all the gods of Egypt I will execute judgment: I am the LORD.**

Jesus is the first born son of every person that has ever lived on earth. We were created in the image and likeness of Jesus and the Father. Jesus was created by the father before the foundation of the world. Therefore everything about Jesus was already in the father before he was beggotten and exalted. Jesus was exalted because of his humility and obedience in heaven. Lucifer/Satan was demoted because of his pride, lust, coveteousness, and disobedience.

The first born son has the ordained responsibility of recieving the inheritance of his father. Jesus Christ recieved the inheritance of the Father which is power, authority and the souls of his children. When the first born son is in the will of God, the family can have a leader that preserves the way to allow the rest of the family a way to be saved from destruction. When the first born son is out of order, the rest of the family suffers. Time and resources are wasted. Negative influences take over, and the entire nation falls for the lack of good examples. Jesus Christ came to be an example. Children are more influenced by their peers than their parents most of the time. The first born son becomes a leader and peer of all other children.

**Romans 8:29** says, "For whom he did foreknow, he also did predestinate to be conformed to the image of his Son, that he might be the firstborn among many brethren."

The angels in heaven are children of the Father that make a brotherhood, and the children of the Father on earth make a brotherhood including women. The mystery of the Bride of Christ (the brotherhood) is that women were created to become one with one man as the man was created to be one with Jesus. Jesus is the head of the body. The man is the head of the woman. The head controls all of the members of the body. The man controls all of the wives that have become one with him. This way, the man can become fruitful and produce more citizens for the kingdom of God. When a nation of people are enslaved by a system that requires much time and energy to obain resources for survival, no wife or one wife is recomended for leaders and teachers in the kingdom of God. Leaders in the kingdom of God don't have time to be distracted by the cares of the world and how he may please his wife when his servitude is extremely important to uphold the order of God. King David was a priest with serveral wives, but look how much trouble the lust of one woman got him in.

A child lets a woman know how she makes her husband feel. The woman lets her husband know how he makes God feel. Women are angry because they are the main physical representatives of God to show men that we have disconnected from the source of order. When men are in order, women have no choice but to be in order, because every man will be obligated keep them in order. The lust of men has allowed the power (sexuality) of women to cause men to forget about God.

A man of God will care more about what a woman puts in her body than what she puts on her body. The woman's body has to grow the seed that the man planted in her womb (a matrix). If the woman's body is disfunctional, the child will be born incomplete and in a deficit. Everything we taste, smell, feel, see and hear can get into the heart (pineal gland) and body. A woman's father has the responsibility of keeping the woman from seeing, hearing, feeling, smelling, and tasting the things that will be harmful to the seed of her husband to come. When a woman is married, her husband takes on the responsibility of keeping the woman form seeing, hearing, feeling, smelling, and tasting things that will be harmful to his children.

Women are always thinking, so their thoughts turn into words. Children need an abundance of stimuli, so the woman is made to talk to the children all day if she has to. The man is designed to listen to God. When the child needs help, it cries to its mother. When the mother needs help, she cries to her husband. When the man needs help, he cries out to God. God instructs the man. The man instructs the woman. The woman instructs the children. Women are to get their knowledge and instruction from their man and transfer it to the children. When a man of God is absent from the woman, the woman is automatically vulnerable and subject to demonic deception. God covers the man, and the man covers the woman. This is why the serpent could decieve Eve in the garden of Eden. When the man is removed, the order of God is removed. When the first born son is not dedicated to God, demonic influence will have the open door to pervert and destroy the inheritance.

**Revelation 12:7** says, "And there was war in heaven: Michael and his angels fought against the dragon; and the dragon fought and his angels,

8. And prevailed not; neither was their place found any more in heaven.

9. And the great dragon was cast out, that old serpent, called the Devil, and Satan, which deceiveth the whole world: he was cast out into the earth, and his angels were cast out with him."

**Matthew 11:12** says, "And from the days of John the Baptist until now the kingdom of heaven suffereth violence, and the violent take it by force."

**Ephesians 6:12** says, "For we wrestle not against flesh and blood, but against principalities, against powers, against the rulers of the darkness of this world, against spiritual wickedness in high places."

**Matthew 18:18** says, "Verily I say unto you, Whatsoever ye shall bind on earth shall be bound in heaven: and whatsoever ye shall loose on earth shall be loosed in heaven.

# THE MATRIX IN ME

My great grandfather on my dad's side was born in slavery. His name was Isaac. His slave master happened to be a woman because her husband died and left her his slaves. In those days, it was illegal for women to own property. During the civil war, her slaves were captrured in a stockade. She went to get her slaves by herself, and brought them all home. Isaac fell in love with her niece Ann and got her pregnant. Therefore, she got Ann classified as a mulatto so they could get married. In those days there were white skinned black people, and no matter how fair the complexion, black or brown genetics classified a person negro or nigger. It was illegal for white and black people to get married at the time. My great grandfather's slave master was an extraordinary woman with a lot of power and enough of God's love to preserve the genetics of Jacob (Israel) and Esau (Edom) coming together in holy matrimony.

Isaac and Ann gave birth to my grandfather Pleasant and his three sisters. Pleasant raised his sisters as a teenager when Isaac and Ann passed away. Pleasant was a hard worker and a strict disciplinarian. He had compassion and love for people. When he was 27 he witnessed a man being drafted into World War 1. He saw how his family was crying and concerned about their survival considering that their only provider was being taken away. Pleasant saw their situation and volunteered to take his place in the draft. When Pleasant said, "I'll take his place", the recruiter said, "Sure nigger, you can take his place." He went to war and came back without a scratch.

Pleasant saw many unruly women and wanted a woman that didn't have skeletons in her closet. He wanted to settle down and have a family. Pleasant married my grandmother Bernice Jones who was raised in the country and protected by her father. She was an Israelite and Blackfoot Native American, so she had dark skin. He was mixed with Israelite and Edomite, Japhite, or French; so he had fair skin. Pleasant was 44 and Bernice was 24. Pleasant lived to be 106 and outlived his wife Bernice. Together they had six children and one miscarriage. My father Charles Neblett was the middle child. The sister born before him has fair skin, and his brother born after him has fair skin, but Charles has brown skin. His full name is Charles Delbert Neblett, for each name has 7 letters.

My father is a serious person with a lot of pride that came from the spirit of rejection which came from his childhood. He was angry at racism all of his life, but he never read the Bible to see what the will of God was for racism and why God created segregation. All he knew was that Hebrews were black and brown people. Therefore I was born with white skin (like Noah), and God put me in the perfect circumstances to understand the mystery of who we are and why we are here.

My mother Marvinia Jetton Benton Neblett is one of a kind. Her mother Jettie had Israelite and Edomite, Japhite, or what we call European DNA. Marvinia's father was 100% Israelite. Two of my grandparents, of opposite gender, on each opposite side, had some Caucasion DNA. My mother was barren at marriage in 1974, so she fasted and prayed for 10 years to have children, and I opened the matrix in 1984. My birthday is 1/11/84. My parents are both brown skin but I came out with white skin. The rest of my sibblings have brown skin. My brother, which is 18 months younger than me symbolizes Jacob, and I symbolize Esau. I was ordained to understand the nations of Jacob and Esau, which is Edom and Israel.

My grandmother Jettie suffered from demonic attacts at her family care home. Mama almost were overcome by the same demons. She was crying nonstop on her porch when a woman handed her a Bible and told her to read everything Jesus said in red. As she was reading she could feel the Holy Spirit traveling through the cells of her body removing all the darkness. Every since then, she holds on to God everyday and depends on the Holy Spirit for everything. Mama writes a lot as a God-given sign to me that my gift is writing and documenting what God wants his people to know. WE DONT WRESTLE AGAINST FLESH AND BLOOD.

I opened the matrix, because I am the firstborn son and my parents are Israelites. My father Charles Neblett was one of the most faithful and courageous activist in the 1960's human rights movement. He was a foot soldier, SNCC Freedom Singer, and protested at a Ku Klux Klan rally without a gun. Mama Marvinia was raised by a hustler that kept her in the house safe from the Sodom and Gomorrah environment at the time. Her father was mean and abusive so Marvinia isn't scared of anybody. My mother went to church at a young age and got saved. God made sure my mother married my father to keep him from trouble. My mother is a gangster for Jesus Christ. She loves her enemies, and spreads love even when its uninvited. She wakes up every morning singing praises to God, and when she has bad thoughts she gets to rebuking and binding evil spirits that try to come against her. They both have dedicated their life for the elevation of God's chosen people in the face of poverty. They didn't keep a television in the house, and they focused on education. The weapons of this warfare are not carnal. I'm the one ordained to break the curse and edify the church.

I'm silly enough to asked God for a super hero name since he wanted me to speak to the people. He said that I already have the best name. Khary means 'He who walks with God', but since you wanna be funny, how about 'Redneck Hebrew to tha Rescue'. How Bout Dat!!! Be careful what you ask for. God has a sense of humor!!!

# GLORY TO GOD

**Lord you are the author and finisher, creator, giver of life and taker of life, God of wrath, but full of mercy, full of grace, executer of righteous judgment, corrector of those you love, vengeance belongs to you, love is your essence, all powerful, wonderful, amazing, awesome, incredible, & marvelous. With your infinite wisdom you put forth events in motion so that you get the glory in the end, and that your will be done in stripping the pride from man, so we may be humble; for by humility is the only way we can be what we were created to be. Obedient and grateful children to you father.**

**Numbers 23:19 says, "God is not a man, that he should lie; neither the son of man, that he should repent: hath he said, and shall he not do it? or hath he spoken, and shall he not make it good?"**

Lucifer the great red dragon and his followers fell from heaven because of pride, and you have given man the opportunity to lose pride and become servants of your will. Lucifer lost his first estate, and now earth is his second estate. Earth is our first estate, and because you gave your only begotten son as the last blood sacrifice, we have the opportunity to graduate to our second estate as the Bride of Christ. Salvation can only come from you and not of man, lest any man should boast.

**Revelation 12:7** says, "And there was war in heaven: Michael and his angels fought against the dragon; and the dragon fought and his angels,

8. And prevailed not; neither was their place found any more in heaven.

9. And the great dragon was cast out, that old serpent, called the Devil, and Satan, which deceiveth the whole world: he was cast out into the earth, and his angels were cast out with him.

10. And I heard a loud voice saying in heaven, Now is come salvation, and strength, and the kingdom of our God, and the power of his Christ: for the accuser of our brethren is cast down, which accused them before our God day and night."

**Isaiah 14:13** says, "For thou hast said in thine heart, I will ascend into heaven, I will exalt my throne above the stars of God: I will sit also upon the mount of the congregation, in the sides of the north."

***In the beginning, the angels of God that were expelled from Heaven thought they could corrupt the genetics of the entire creation on earth. The fallen angels were appointed a redemptive task of protecting and guiding man in the righteous ways of God, but they made a covenant together to take women for wives, corrupt the DNA of creation, and teach them ways that lead to death. They wanted to create their own world on earth, and take the glory that belongs the Most High God for their own. If they would have succeeded, Jesus wouldn't have had a pure bloodline to come through.***

**Genesis 3:15** says, "And I will put enmity between thee and the woman, and between thy seed and her seed; it shall bruise thy head, and thou shalt bruise his heel."

They genetically modified plants and animals, and had children with women. As Judgement, you cast them into hell to be reserved until judgment. You repented in your heart that you made man on Earth, because man's flesh was too weak to resist the seduction and deception of the Devil.

**Genesis 6:6** says, "And it repented the Lord that he had made man on the earth, and it grieved him at his heart."

LORD you preserved your creation through the perfect DNA of Noah's family, and has given man a chance to inhabit eternal paradise. **You have given your only begotten son, so that whoever believes in him will not parish, but have everlasting life.** Everything you made is compatible to your spirit, for your spirit is life. You are the way, truth, and life.

**Genesis 6** says, "And it came to pass, when men began to multiply on the face of the earth, and daughters were born unto them,

**2. That the sons of God saw the daughters of men that they were fair; and they took them wives of all which they chose.**

3. And the Lord said, My spirit shall not always strive with man, for that he also is flesh: yet his days shall be an hundred and twenty years.

**4. There were giants in the earth in those days; and also after that, when the sons of God came in unto the daughters of men, and they bare children to them, the same became mighty men which were of old, men of renown.**

**5. And GOD saw that the wickedness of man was great in the earth, and that every imagination of the thoughts of his heart was only evil continually.**

8. But Noah found grace in the eyes of the Lord.

9. These are the generations of Noah: Noah was a just man and **perfect in his generations**, and Noah walked with God.

***Noah was perfect in his genes (generations). He didn't have any DNA of the Fallen Angels, and he walked with God, so his family was able to repopulate the Earth.***

**2 Peter 2:4-5** says, "For if God spared not the angels that sinned, but cast them down to hell, and delivered them into chains of darkness, to be reserved unto judgment; And spared not the old world, but saved Noah the eighth person, a preacher of righteousness, bringing in the flood upon the world of the ungodly." **(Hell is inside the earth, but exists as a spiritual dimension. Jail without electricity food and water is what hell is like, and the magma, lava, or molten rock inside earth is what the Lake of Fire is like. There are levels inside the earth with tunnels and caves. Most of the fallen angels are reptilian and reptiles need heat to regulate their body temperature. They are cold blooded. When angels are banished from Heaven, they lose their glorified body and take on a less glorified body compatible to the environment. This is why they could procreate with their DNA.)**

**As in Matthew 20, you do what you will with what belongs to you.** The work of your right hand is seen in your creation. You have saved us by your strong arm. Jesus sits at the right hand of the Father. Jesus is called "The Word of

God" in heaven. All things were spoken into existence by "The Word", and the Holy Spirit manifested and materialized the world we live in. The Spirit and the Father is one within all living things maintaining life according to his established law, recording everything from thoughts, words, and actions. This is why blaspheming the Holy Ghost is an unforgivable sin. **Therefore, all things were created by The Word, for The Word.**

**Colossians 2:2-3** "That their hearts might be comforted, being knit together in love, and unto all riches of the full assurance of understanding, to the acknowledgement of the mystery of God, and of the Father, and of Christ;"

"In whom are hid all the treasures of wisdom and knowledge."

**John 1:1** says, "In the beginning was the Word, and the Word was with God, and the Word was God."

**John 1:14** says, "And the Word was made flesh, and dwelt among us, (and we beheld his glory, the glory as of the only begotten of the Father,) full of grace and truth."

**Revelation 19:13** says, "And he was clothed with a vesture dipped in blood: and his name is called The Word of God."

**Hebrews 2:6-10** says, "For unto the angels hath he not put in subjection the world to come, whereof we speak

6. But one in a certain place testified, saying, What is man, that thou art mindful of him? or the son of man that thou visitest him?

7. Thou madest him a little lower than the angels; thou crownedst him with glory and honour, and didst set him over the works of thy hands:

8. Thou hast put all things in subjection under his feet. For in that he put all in subjection under him, he left nothing that is not put under him. But now we see not yet all things put under him.

9. But we see Jesus, who was made a little lower than the angels for the suffering of death, crowned with glory and honour; that he by the grace of God should taste death for every man.

10. For it became him, for whom are all things, and by whom are all things, in bringing many sons unto glory, to make the captain of their salvation perfect through sufferings.

**Revelation 4:11** says, "Thou art worthy, O Lord, to receive glory and honour and power: for thou hast created all things, and for thy pleasure they are and were created."

**1 Corinthians 8:6** says, "But to us there is but **one God, the Father, of whom are all things, and we in him**; and **one Lord Jesus Christ, by whom are all things, and we by him**."

**1 Corinthians 15:22** says, "For as in Adam all die, even so in Christ shall all be made alive."

**Colossians 3:11** says, "Where there is neither Greek nor Jew, circumcision nor uncircumcision, Barbarian, Scythian, bond nor free: but Christ is all, and in all."

***Everything on Earth is symbolism of something that is in Heaven.***

**Genesis 1:26** says, "And God said, Let us make man in our image, after our likeness: and let them have dominion over the fish of the sea, and over the fowl of the air, and over the cattle, and over all the earth, and over every creeping thing that creepeth upon the earth.

**Matthew 6:10** says, "Thy kingdom come, Thy will be done in earth, as it is in heaven."

**Matthew 18:18** says, "Verily I say unto you, Whatsoever ye shall bind on earth shall be bound in heaven: and whatsoever ye shall loose on earth shall be loosed in heaven."

**The Father Yah (God) has seven spirits. All of the Spirits of Yah (God) have operations throughout his creation. However, man is in need of the Holy Spirit. In the book of Enoch, God is reffered to as the Father of Spirits. The Holy Ghost is God, and when Jesus died for our sins, he did so to send the Holy Ghost as a comforter to all those that believe. Water baptism is the symbolization of being born again.**

**Revelation 5:6** says, "And I beheld, and, lo, in the midst of the throne and of the four beasts, and in the midst of the elders, stood a Lamb as it had been slain, having seven horns and seven eyes, which are the seven Spirits of God sent forth into all the earth.

**Revelation 4:5** says, "And out of the throne proceeded lightnings and thunderings and voices: and there were seven lamps of fire burning before the throne, which are the seven Spirits of God."

**Revelation 3:1** says, "And unto the angel of the church in Sardis write; These things saith he that hath the seven Spirits of God, and the seven stars; I know thy works, that thou hast a name that thou livest, and art dead."

**Revelation 1:4** says, "John to the seven churches which are in Asia: Grace be unto you, and peace, from him which is, and which was, and which is to come; and from the seven Spirits which are before his throne."

**Satan Can Only Immitated The Father For He Is Not Origional**

**Luke 8:2** says, "And certain women, which had been healed of evil spirits and infirmities, Mary called Magdalene, out of whom went seven devils.

**Luke 11:26** says, "Then goeth he, and taketh to him seven other spirits more wicked than himself; and they enter in, and dwell there: and the last state of that man is worse than the first."

The Holy Ghost is what keeps the genetics of man undefiled. There are only two unforgivable sins; blaspheming the Holy Ghost, and taking the mark of the beast. The mark of the beast is technology that will control the monetary system. The mark of the beast, and/or not having the Holy Ghost will result in defiled genetics. By this, people are automatically subject to demonic possession. Sin and demonic possession is what defiles the DNA of a man. We are born in sin, shapen in iniquity, and inherit generational curses. The sins of our parents fall on us fulfilling the law, 'reap what you sow.' **That's why we have to be born again by the Holy Ghost in the name of Jesus Christ (the Messiah) to get God's DNA. Not of corruptible seed but incorruptible seed. The Holy Ghost**

**is eternal, and what's impossible for man is highly possible for God.**

**1 Corinthians 15:45** says, "And so it is written, The first man Adam was made a living soul; the last Adam was made a quickening spirit."

**1 Peter 1:23** says, "Being born again, not of corruptible seed, but of incorruptible, by the word of God, which liveth and abideth for ever."

**Romans 1:20 says,** "For the invisible things of him from the creation of the world are clearly seen, being understood by the things that are made, even his eternal power and Godhead; so that we are without excuse: Because that, when they knew God, they glorified him not as God, neither were thankful; but became vain in their imaginations, and their foolish heart was darkened." **(When man knew God, they had pride against God, so he has withdrawn his face for us to have faith. He have never left us or forsaken us. We have the task of seeking God's face.)**

**2 Chronicles 7:14** says, "If my people, which are called by my name, shall humble themselves, and pray, and seek my face, and turn from their wicked ways; then will I hear from heaven, and will forgive their sin, and will heal their land." **(Humility is the first step)**

***Life is a real test, but you have given us your word, testimonies, and the witness of your prophecy so that we have no excuse. Some of us know you because you have answered prayers, and reached out revealing your existence.***

**John 20:29** says, "Jesus saith unto him, Thomas, because thou hast seen me, thou hast believed: blessed are they that have not seen, and yet have believed."

***You have written your law in our hearts, so that we innately know when we are in sin.***

**Hebrews 8:10** says, "For this is the covenant that I will make with the house of Israel after those days, saith the Lord; I will put my laws into their mind, and write them in their hearts: and I will be to them a God, and they shall be to me a people."

***You preserve the seed of the righteous. You have ordained some to believe, but allow the seed of the wicked one to eat the fruit of their doings.***

**Romans 8:29-31** says, "For whom he did foreknow, he also did predestinate to be conformed to the image of his Son that he might be the firstborn among many brethren. Moreover whom he did predestinate, them he also called: and whom he called, them he also justified: and whom he justified, them he also glorified. What shall we then say to these things? If God be for us, who can be against us?

**Proverbs 1:24-33** says, "Because I have called, and ye refused; I have stretched out my hand, and no man regarded;

25. But ye have set at nought all my counsel, and would none of my reproof:

26. I also will laugh at your calamity; I will mock when your fear cometh;

27. When your fear cometh as desolation, and your destruction cometh as a whirlwind; when distress and anguish cometh upon you.

28. Then shall they call upon me, but I will not answer; they shall seek me early, but they shall not find me:

29. For that they hated knowledge, and did not choose the fear of the LORD:

30. They would none of my counsel: they despised all my reproof.

31. Therefore shall they eat of the fruit of their own way, and be filled with their own devices.

32. For the turning away of the simple shall slay them, and the prosperity of fools shall destroy them.

33. But whoso hearkeneth unto me shall dwell safely, and shall be quiet from fear of evil.

**Jeremiah 21:14** says, "But I will punish you according to the fruit of your doings, saith the Lord: and I will kindle a fire in the forest thereof, and it shall devour all things round about it."

***You have no respect of persons, and require obedience from all men. You have mercy on whom you will have mercy, and you have favor on whomever according to your will.***

**Romans 9:15** says, "For he saith to Moses, I will have mercy on whom I will have mercy, and I will have compassion on whom I will have compassion."

**Romans 4:3-8** says, "For what saith the scripture? Abraham believed God, and it was counted unto him for righteousness. Now to him that worketh is the reward not reckoned of grace, but of debt. But to him that worketh not, but believeth on him that justifieth the ungodly, his faith is counted for righteousness. Even as David also describeth the blessedness of the man, unto whom God imputeth righteousness without works, Saying, Blessed are they whose iniquities are forgiven, and whose sins are covered. Blessed is the man to whom the Lord will not impute sin."

**2 Peter 2:6 & 9** says, "And turning the cities of Sodom and Gomorrah into ashes condemned them with an overthrow, making them an example unto those that after should live ungodly." The Lord knoweth how to deliver the godly out of temptations, and to reserve the unjust unto the day of judgment to be punished."

**Psalm 30:5** says, "For his anger endureth but a moment; in his favour is life: weeping may endure for a night, but joy cometh in the morning."

**Psalm 30:7** says, "Lord, by thy favour thou hast made my mountain to stand strong: thou didst hide thy face, and I was troubled."

**Proverbs 22:1** says, "A good name is rather to be chosen than great riches, and loving favour rather than silver and gold."

***You have established the bounds for creation; life and death, gift and curse, sowing and reaping, redemption and condemnation, law and grace, rising and falling, graduation and giving up, master and servant, freedom and bondage, reward and punishment, light and darkness, good and evil.***

**You said, "My sheep hear my voice, and I know them, and they follow me." You made two main colors for sheep, which are black and white. Brown and grey is in between white and black. When sheep hair is white, the skin can be black. When sheep hair is black, the skin can be white.** You made sheep hair nappy, and when it gets long it locks up. You created the black man. Then you created the white man out of the black man. The black man was the first rulers of the world. Then you allowed the white man to rule the world.

**Job 30:30** says, "**My skin is black** upon me, and my bones are burned with heat."

**Song of Solomon 1:5** says, "**I am black**, but comely, O ye daughters of Jerusalem, as the tents of Kedar, as the curtains of Solomon."

**Song of Solomon 1:6** says, "Look not upon me, because **I am black…**"

**Song of Solomon 5:11** says, "His head is as the most fine gold, **his locks (dread locks) are bushy**, and **black** as a raven."

**Jeremiah 14:2** says, "Judah mourneth, and the gates thereof languish; they are **black unto the ground** (black as black soil); and the cry of Jerusalem is gone up."

**Jeremiah 14:2** says, "…they are **black unto the ground** (black as black soil)..."

**Lamentations 4:8** says, "**Their visage is blacker than a coal**; they are not known in the streets: their skin cleaveth to their bones; it is withered, it is become like a stick."

**Lamentations 5:10** says, "**Our skin was black** like an oven because of the terrible famine."

**Joel 2:6** says, "Before their face the people shall be much pained: **all faces shall gather blackness**."

**Nahum 2:10** says, "...the **faces of them all gather blackness**."

**A Leper is an Albino...Leprous is White Spots...Leprosy is White with the Disease (Red Boils Like Herpes).**

**2 Kings 5:27** says, "The **leprosy** therefore of Naaman shall **cleave unto thee**, and **unto thy seed for ever**. And he went out from his presence **a leper** as **white as snow**."

**Numbers 12:10** says, "And the cloud departed from off the tabernacle , and, behold, **Miriam became leprous, white as snow**: and Aaron looked upon Miriam, and behold, she was leprous."

**Genesis 4:11-12** says, "And now art thou **cursed from the earth**, which hath opened her mouth to receive thy brother's blood from thy hand. 12. When thou tillest the ground, **it shall not henceforth yield unto thee her strength**; a **fugitive** and a **vagabond** shalt thou be in the earth." **(Man was created from the soil of the earth. Rich soil is black soil, and because of the pride in various people, God cursed the black soil they were created from to white striping out all the minerals (melanin). This is why God considered Lepers unclean because their weakened immune system subjected them to disease. There is no white soil. There is white sand or rock which represents calcification or hardness of heart. The darker**

**the soil, the softer it is symbolizing softness of heart. When the soil is soft, a seed can grow and sprout up through the ground. When the soil is hard the seed is unable to sprout. The soil symbolizes the heart, and some black people who had hard hearts were cursed white as a leper. The land of Europe and Russia doesn't yeild the strengh of southern lands. This is why the main concern of Europeans was to find herbs and spices for medicine. The lack of immunity of their body correlated to the lack of medicine in the earth.)**

***For The Sin Of Pride God Removed The Melanin From Skin***

***God Knew From The Foundation Of The World That He Would Create White Men From The Black Man To Show All Men That Pride Comes Before The Fall***

***White Skin Is A Physical Representation Of Spiritual Pride***

***Pride Was Passed Down From Satan To The Black Man And God Made White Men From Prideful Black Men***

***God Took The Rib From A Black Man (Adam) & Created A Black Woman (Eve). Then Took The Pride In The Black Man & Created A White Man***

***The Creation Of The White Man Was A Miracle***

**Exodus 4:6** says, "And the Lord said furthermore unto him, Put now thine hand into thy bosom. And he put his hand into his bosom: and when he took it out, behold, his hand was leprous as snow. **(God was letting Moses know**

**he had the power to turn a man's skin white as snow. None of Pharaoh's magicians had the power to do that).**

**2 Kings 5:27** says, "**The leprosy therefore of Naaman shall cleave unto thee, and unto thy seed for ever**. And he went out from his presence a **leper as white as snow**." (Those that inherit the genetic traits of white skin have so because of the leper gene of their for-fathers. '**Albino**' is the modern term for the biblical term '**Leper**'.

**The White Man Fulfils God's Will By Compelling The Children Of God to Humble Themselves**

**Genesis 25:23** says, "And the LORD said unto her, **Two nations** are in thy womb, and **two manner** of people shall be separated from thy bowels; and the **one people shall be stronger than the other people; and the elder shall serve the younger.**

24. And when her days to be delivered were fulfilled, behold, there were twins in her womb.

25. And the first came out red, all over like an hairy garment; and they called his name Esau." **(Neanderthal DNA is Edomite DNA.)**

**Genesis 25:30** says, "And **Esau** said to Jacob, Feed me, I pray thee, with that same **red pottage**; for I am faint: therefore was his name called **Edom**." **(The red pottage was bloody meat. Edomites like to eat their meat bloody like medium rare steak.)**

**Leviticus 17:12** says, "Therefore I said unto the children of Israel, **No soul of you shall eat blood, neither shall any stranger that sojourneth among you eat blood.**"

**Deuteronomy 12:23** says, "Only be sure that thou **eat not the blood: for the blood is the life; and thou mayest not eat the life with the flesh.**"

**Leviticus 17:14** says, "For it is the life of all flesh; the blood of it is for the life thereof: therefore I said unto the children of Israel, **Ye shall eat the blood of no manner of flesh:** for the life of all flesh is the blood thereof: **whosoever eateth it shall be cut off.**"

**Amos 1:9** says, "Thus saith the LORD; For three transgressions of Tyrus, and for four, I will not turn away the punishment thereof; **because they delivered up the whole captivity to Edom, and remembered not the brotherly covenant.**"

**Deuteronomy 28:49-50** says, "The LORD shall bring a nation against thee from far, from the end of the earth, as swift as the eagle flieth; a nation whose tongue thou shalt not understand; A nation of fierce countenance, which shall not regard the person of the old, nor shew favour to the young."

**You said, "But many that are first shall be last; and the last shall be first." You have chosen the foolish things to confound the wise, and have chosen the weak things to confound the things that are mighty. You kept your covenant with Abraham to preserve and multiply his seed. You protected Israel from being wiped out by scattering them all over the earth and subjecting Israel to servitude. By this Israel has been multiplied and preserved. Moreover, Israel has blessed all nations with their labor, culture, salt and uniqueness. Your thoughts are not our thoughts, neither your ways our ways. Who you love, you correct, and slavery is a sign of correction as a father to a son in whom You delight.**

**Proverbs 3:12** says, "For whom the Lord loveth he correcteth; even as a father the son in whom he delighteth."

**Genesis 26:4** says, "And I will make thy seed to multiply as the stars of heaven, and will give unto thy seed all these countries; and in thy seed shall all the nations of the earth be blessed."

**Genesis 15:13** says, "And he said unto Abram, Know of a surety that thy seed shall be a stranger in a land that is not theirs, and shall serve them; and they shall afflict them four hundred years."

**Slavery was the vehicle in which Abraham's seed was multiplied all over the earth.** Slaves are resources and natural resources are of ultimate value when they can reproduce. The Hebrew slaves built the foundation of our society today, and have shown the world their excellence through music, every physical activity, intellectual activity, spirituality, and ability to survive the worst conditions known to man and still forgive their enemy/oppressor to the point they take on the oppressor's ways. **(Skinny Jeans)**

**Proverbs 3:31** says, **"Envy thou not the oppressor, and choose none of his ways."**

Slavery was also a catalyst for humility. The anointing is multiplied, and the soul is preserved through humility. **Belief in you was necessary for the Israelites to enter the Promise Land, and belief is necessary for us to get to New Jerusalem, which is the New Promise Land. Jerusalem is the land, Israel is the people. 'Land of Israel' simply means the land that belongs to 'Israel the people'.**

**Luke 21:24** says, "And they shall fall by the edge of the sword, and shall be led away captive into all nations: and **Jerusalem shall be trodden down of the Gentiles, until the times of the Gentiles be fulfilled**." **(The people that are in Jerusalem today are Gentiles (Khazars). Israel has been scattered by slavery and migration.)**

**Ashkenazi Jews claim to be Semetic (Shemetic). Abraham came from the bloodline of Shem. Ashkenaz was the son of Gomer, and Gomer was the son of Japheth. Noah had three sons: Shem, Ham, and Japheth. Japheth's bloodline evolved into white people.**

**Revelation 2:9** says, "I know thy works, and tribulation, and poverty, (but thou art rich) and I know the blasphemy of them which say they are Jews, and are not, but are the synagogue of Satan."

**Revelation 3:9** says, "Behold, I will make them of the synagogue of Satan, which say they are Jews, and are not, but do lie; behold, I will make them to come and worship before thy feet, and to know that I have loved thee."

Amos 9:11-12 says, "In that day will I raise up the tabernacle of David that is fallen, and close up the breaches thereof; and I will raise up his ruins, and I will build it as in the days of old."

12. That they may possess the remnant of Edom, and of all the heathen, which are called by my name, saith the LORD that doeth this. **(Durring the one thousand year reign on earth with Jesus Christ, the remnant of the elder (Esau) will serve the younger (Jacob).**

**Jeremiah 29:18** says, "And I will persecute them with the sword, with the famine, and with the pestilence, and will deliver them to be removed to all the kingdoms of the earth, to be a **curse**, and an **astonishment**, and an **hissing**, and **reproach**, among **all the nations whither I have driven them**."

**Deuteronomy 28:37** says, "And thou shalt become an astonishment, a proverb, and a byword, among all nations whither the Lord shall lead thee. **(The byword is NIGGER)**

**1Kings 9:7** says, "…and Israel shall be a proverb and a byword (nigger) among all people:"

**Psalm 44:14** says, "Thou makest us a **byword among the heathen, a shaking of the head among the people**." **(As you can see, there is a huge problem within the black neighborhood all over the world, and other nationalities just shake their heads; nevertheless, African Americans (Hebrew Israelites) are an astonishment above all other people).**

**Deuteronomy 28:64** says, "And the Lord shall scatter thee among all people, from the one end of the earth even unto the other and there thou shalt server other gods, which neither thou nor thy fathers have known, even wood and stone." **(Islam - Kabba Stone & Catholicism - Every Graven Image...Cesare Borgia was painted as the image of Jesus Christ.)**

**Deuteronomy 28:68** says "And the LORD shall bring thee into Egypt (America) again with ships, by the way whereof I spake unto thee, Thou shalt see it no more again: and there ye shall be sold unto your enemies for bondmen and bondwomen, and no man shall buy you ('buy you' means 'buy your freedom')." **(The Americas is the Second Egypt. A demonic place of bondage, affliction, and**

**wickedness. 400 Years of slavery in Egypt and Americas - 1619 to 2019). The year of 2020 was a strong delusion.**

**2 Thessalonians 2:10-11** says, **"And with all deceivableness of unrighteousness in them that perish; because they received not the love of the truth, that they might be saved.**

**11. And for this cause God shall send them strong delusion, that they should believe a lie:**

**The Human Rights Movement or the Civil Rights Movement, in America, was by the hand of God to show everyone the difference between pride and humility. The Nation of Islam and black power movement represented pride. Dr. King and the non-violent movement represented humility. By humility progress was made. Most African Americans are Hebrews. You put the will to fight oppression in the hearts of certain people to bring the change of times, which was a part of your will. Dr. Martin Luther King Jr. was a prophet for the season at hand. Many suffered and died, but nothing good comes without sacrifice. My father was a soldier for the Hebrews in the civil rights movement, and for the faith of my mother, you gave me the gift of understanding for the people. Everything about me is a witness to the fact. I'm the first born, and resemble every nationality of people on the face of the earth.**

**Romans 3:1-2** says, "What advantage then hath the Jew? or what profit is there of circumcision? Much every way: chiefly, because that unto them were committed the oracles of God."

**Romans 9:4** says, "Who are Israelites; to whom pertaineth the adoption, and the glory, and the covenants, and the giving of the law, and the service of God, and the promises."

**Amos 3:2** says, **"You only have I known of all the families of the earth: therefore I will punish you for all your iniquities."**

**Ephesians 1:5** says, "Having predestinated us unto the adoption of children by Jesus Christ to himself, according to the good pleasure of his will."

**Romans 2:29** says, "But he is a Jew, which is one inwardly; and circumcision is that of the heart, in the spirit, and not in the letter; whose praise is not of men, but of God."

**Romans 2:9** says, "Tribulation and anguish, upon every soul of man that doeth evil, of the Jew first, and also of the Gentile;"

**Romans 2:10** says, "But glory, honour, and peace, to every man that worketh good, to the Jew first, and also to the Gentile:"

**Anyone that is covered by the blood of Jesus is in the bloodline. Disobedience to God breaks the bloodline, because Abraham was faithful and obedient to God. You are the same yesterday, today, and forever. Without the shedding of blood, there is no remission of sin. That's why we have to believe in the last blood sacrifice, which is your Son Jesus Christ. However, we still have to make a sacrifice, and that sacrifice is fasting and prayer.**

**Matthew 17:21** says, **"Howbeit this kind goeth not out but by prayer and fasting."**

**Isaiah 58:6** says, "Is not this the fast that I have chosen? to loose the bands of wickedness, to undo the heavy burdens, and to let the oppressed go free, and that ye break every yoke?"

**Matthew 6:16-17** says, "Moreover when ye fast, be not, as the hypocrites, of a sad countenance: for they disfigure their faces, that they may appear unto men to fast. Verily I say unto you, They have their reward. But thou, when thou fastest, anoint thine head, and wash thy face; **(Jesus said "When ye fast", not "If you fast")**

***You have set before us to either suffer for evil, or for good. All is vanity and vexation of spirit, but your word is life and health to all flesh. It is your spirit that quickeneth, but the flesh profits nothing.***

**1 Peter 3:17** says, "For it is better, if the will of God be so, that ye suffer for well doing, than for evil doing."

**Revelation 13:7** says, "And it was given unto him to make war with the saints, and to overcome them: and power was given him over all kindreds, and tongue and nations."

**Hebrews 2:10** says, "For it became him, for whom are all things, and by whom are all things in bringing many sons unto glory, to make the captain of their salvation perfect through sufferings."

**1Peter 5:10** says, "But the God of all grace, who hath called us unto his eternal glory by Christ Jesus, after that ye have suffered a while, make you perfect, stablish, strengthen, settle you."

**1Peter 3:18** says, "For Christ also hath once suffered for our sins, the just for the unjust, that he might bring us to

God, being put to death in the flesh, but quickened by the Spirit.

***Your interest is to seek out the heart of man to see who will lose self-will and pride to be a vessel of your will. Who will seek after your ways? Who will understand? Who will lose one's life to find your life, which is eternal life? Who will make their body a living sacrifice? Who will be totally dependent on you like a child depends on a father? Who will store treasure in heaven? Who will believe in what is not seen, more than what is seen? Who will accept what is allowed? Who has eyes to see? Who will endure till the end?**

**Matthew 10:22** says, "And ye shall be hated of all men for my name's sake: but he that endureth to the end shall be saved."

**For the invisible things of you, from the creation of the world, are clearly seen, being understood by the things that are made, even your eternal power and Godhead, so that we are without excuse.***

**Psalm 95:10** says, "Forty years long was I grieved with this generation, and said, It is a people that do err in their heart, and they have not known my ways."

**Jeremiah 8:6** says, "I hearkened and heard, but they spake not aright: no man repented him of his wickedness, saying, What have I done? every one turned to his course, as the horse rusheth into the battle."

**Jeremiah 6:13** says, "For from the least of them even unto the greatest of them every one is given to covetousness; and from the prophet even unto the priest every one dealeth falsely. They have healed also the hurt of the daughter of my people slightly, saying, Peace, peace; when there is no peace."

**Ecclesiastes 7:20** says, "For there is not a just man upon earth, that doeth good, and sinneth not."

**Matthew 19:17** says, "And he said unto him, Why callest thou me good? there is none good but one, that is, God: but if thou wilt enter into life, keep the commandments."

**Daniel 5:12** says, "Forasmuch as an excellent spirit, and knowledge, and understanding, interpretation of dreams, and shewing of hard sentences, and dissolving of doubts, were found in the same Daniel, whom the king named Belteshazzar: now let Daniel be called, and he will shew the interpretation."

**Genesis 5:24** says, "And Enoch walked with God: and he was not; for God took him."

**Acts 13:22** says, "And when he had removed him, he raised up unto them David to be their king; to whom also he gave their testimony, and said, I have found David the son of Jesse, a man after mine own heart, which shall fulfil all my will."

**James 2:23** says, "And the scripture was fulfilled which saith, Abraham believed God, and it was imputed unto him for righteousness: and he was called the Friend of God."

**Psalm 119:169** says, "Let my cry come near before thee, O Lord: give me understanding according to thy word."

**Proverbs 1:5** says, "A wise man will hear, and will increase learning; and a man of understanding shall attain unto wise counsels."

**Proverbs 4:7** says, "Wisdom is the principal thing; therefore get wisdom: and with all thy getting get understanding."

**Proverbs 28:11** says, "The rich man is wise in his own conceit; but the poor that hath understanding searcheth him out."

**Proverbs 9:6** says, "Forsake the foolish, and live; and go in the way of understanding."

**Proverbs 15:14** says, "The heart of him that hath understanding seeketh knowledge: but the mouth of fools feedeth on foolishness."

**Proverbs 15:32** says, "He that refuseth instruction despiseth his own soul: but he that heareth reproof getteth understanding."

**Proverbs 16:16** says, "How much better is it to get wisdom than gold! and to get understanding rather to be chosen than silver."

**Proverbs 16:22** says, "Understanding is a wellspring of life unto him that hath it: but the instruction of fools is folly."

**Proverbs 17:24** says, "Wisdom is before him that hath understanding; but the eyes of a fool are in the ends of the earth."

**Proverbs 17:27** says, "He that hath knowledge spareth his words: and a man of understanding is of an excellent spirit."

**Proverbs 18:2** says, "A fool hath no delight in understanding, but that his heart may discover itself."

**Proverbs 19:25** says, "Smite a scorner, and the simple will beware: and reprove one that hath understanding, and he will understand knowledge."

**Proverbs 28:2** says, "For the transgression of a land many are the princes (demons) thereof: but by a man of understanding and knowledge the state thereof shall be prolonged."

**Proverbs 24:3** says, "Through wisdom is an house builded; and by understanding it is established."

**Proverbs 28:16** says, "The prince that wanteth understanding is also a great oppressor: but he that hateth covetousness shall prolong his days."

**Proverbs 21:30** says, "There is no wisdom nor understanding nor counsel against the Lord."

**Proverbs 23:23** says, "Buy the truth, and sell it not; also wisdom, and instruction, and understanding."

**Ecclesiastes 3:11** says, "He hath made every thing beautiful in his time: also he hath set the world in their heart, so that no man can find out the work that God maketh from the beginning to the end."

**Romans 11:25** says, "For I would not, brethren, that ye should be ignorant of this mystery, lest ye should be wise in your own conceits; that blindness in part is happened to Israel, until the fulness of the Gentiles be come in."

**Ecclesiastes 3:14-15** says, "I know that, whatsoever God doeth, it shall be for ever: nothing can be put to it, nor any thing taken from it: and God doeth it, that men should fear before him. That which hath been is now; and that which is to be hath already been; and God requireth that which is past."

**Ecclesiastes 7:13** says, "Consider the work of God: for who can make that straight, which he hath made crooked?

**Romans 3:1-2** says, "What advantage then hath the Jew? or what profit is there of circumcision? Much every way: chiefly, because that unto them were committed the oracles of God."

**Revelation 2:9** says, "I know thy works, and tribulation, and poverty, (but thou art rich) and I know the blasphemy of them which say they are Jews, and are not, but are the synagogue of Satan."

**Isaiah 55:5** says, "Behold, thou shalt call a nation that thou knowest not, and nations that knew not thee shall run unto thee because of the Lord thy God, and for the Holy One of Israel; for he hath glorified thee."

**Revelation 3:9** says, "Behold, I will make them of the synagogue of Satan, which say they are Jews, and are not, but do lie; behold, I will make them to come and worship before thy feet, and to know that I have loved thee."

# NOAH WAS ALBINO

**Enoch 105 KJV:**

1 After a time, my son Methuselah took a wife for his son Lamech. She became pregnant by him, and brought forth a child, the flesh of which was as white as snow, and red as a rose; the hair of his head was white like wool, and long; and his eyes were beautiful when he opened them, he illuminated all the house, like the sun; the whole house abounded with light.

3. And when he was taken from the hand of the midwife, opening also his mouth, he spoke to the Lord of righteousness. Then Lamech his father was afraid of him; and fled away to his own father Mathusala, and said, "I have begotten a son, unlike to other children. He is not human; but, resembling the offspring of the angels of heaven, is of a different nature from ours, being altogether unlike to us.

4. His eyes are bright as the rays of the sun; his countenance glorious, and he looks not as if he belonged to me, but to the angels.

5. I am afraid, lest something miraculous should take place on earth in his days.

6. And now, my father, let me entreat and request you to go to our progenitor Enoch, and to learn from him the truth; for his residence is with the angels.

7. When Mathusala heard the words of his son, he came to me at the etremities of the earth; for he had been informed that I was there: and he cried out.

8. I heard his voice, and went to him saying, Behold, I am here, my son; since thou art come to me.

9. He answered and said, On accound of a great event have I come to thee; and on account of a sight difficult to be comprehended have I approached thee.

10. And now, my father, hear me; for to my son Lamech a child has been born, who resembles not him; and whose nature is not like the nature of man. His color is whiter than snow; he is redder than the the rose; the hair of his head is whiter than white wool; his eyes are like the rays of the sun; and when he opened them he illuminated the whole house.

11. When also he was taken from the hand of the midwife, he opened his mouth, and blessed the Lord of heaven.

12. His father Lamech feared, and fled to me, believing not that the child belonged to him, but that he resebled the angels of heaven. And behold I am come to thee, that thou mightest point out to me the truth.

13. Then I, Enoch, answered and said, The Lord will effect a new thing upon the earth. This have I explained, and seen in a vision. I have shown thee that in the generations of Jared my father. Those who were from heaven disregarded the word of the Lord. Behold they committed crimes; laid aside their class, and intermingled with women. With them also they transgressed; married with them, and begot children.

14. A great destruction therefore shall come upon all the earth; a deluge, a great destruction, shall take place in one year.

15. This child with is born to you shall survive on the earth, and his three sons shall be saved with him. When all mankind who are on earth shall die, he shall be safe.

16. And his posterity shall beget on the earth giants, not spiritual, but carnal upon the earth shall a great punishment be inflicted, and it shall be washed from all corruption. Now therefore inform thy son Lamech, that he who is born is his child in truth; and he shall call his name Noah, for he shall be to you a survivor. He and his children shall be saved from the corruption which shall take place in the world; from all the sin and from all the iniquity which shall be consummated on earth in his days. Afterwards shall greater impiety take place than that which had been before consummated on the earth; for I am acquainted with holy mysteries, which the Lord himself has discovered and explained to me; and which I have read in the tablets of heaven.

17. In them I saw it written, that generation after generation shall transgress, until a righteous race shall arise; until transgression and crime perish from off the earth; until all goodness come upon it.

18. And now, my son, go tell thy son Lamech,

19. That the child which is born is his child in truth; and that there is no deception.

20. When Mathusala heard the word of his father Enoch, who had shown hint every secret thing, he returned with understanding, and called the name of that child Noah; because he was to console the earth on account of all its destruction.

# UNDERSTANDING THE GODHEAD

**Father - Son - Holy Spirit**

**3 in 1**

**Romans 1:19** says, "For the invisible things of God, from the creation of the world, are clearly seen, being understood by the things that are made, even his eternal power and Godhead, so that we are without excuse."

**Water, Land, Sky = 3 in 1. Ocean, lake, river = 3 in 1. Mountain, valley, plain = 3 in 1. We exist in the Troposphere, Stratosphere, and the Mesosphere of the atmosphere which makes 3 in 1. Inside the Earth is Inner Core, Outer Core, and Mantle that makes 3 in 1. Head, Torso, Legs = 3 in 1. Hand, for-arm, upper arm = 3 in 1. Foot, shin, thigh = 3 in 1. 1st, 2nd, and 3rd digit in each finger is 3 in 1. The hair on a man's head connects to a full beard, with the 2 eye brows = 3 in 1. Two eye lashes and one eye brow = 3 in 1. Three air ways for oxygen; two nostrils, and one mouth = 3 in 1. Two nipples and one belly button = 3 in 1. The male genitals is 3 in 1 on the outside, and the Woman genitals is 3 in 1 on the inside. Man, woman, child = 3 in 1. The atom is the building block of everything consisting of the proton, electron, and nucleus which makes = 3 in 1. The eye is the window to the soul that has 3 parts; the white part, colored iris, and the pupil = 3 in 1.**

**Amos 3:3** says, **"Can two walk together, except they be agreed?"**

**Luke 10:2** says, "For I tell you, that many prophets and kings have desired to see those things which ye see, and have not seen them; and to hear those things which ye hear, and have not heard them."

**Matthew 13:13** says, "Therefore speak I to them in parables: because they seeing see not; and hearing they hear not, neither do they understand."

**Matthew 13:15** says, "For this people's heart is waxed gross, and their ears are dull of hearing, and their eyes they have closed; lest at any time they should see with their eyes and hear with their ears, and should understand with their heart, and should be converted, and I should heal them.

The Father and the Son are one by the Spirit of God to establish his will according to the matrix we exist in. The Holy Spirit is one of seven spirits of The Father. The Son is 'The Word of God' because the words Jesus speak are spirit. When creation was spoke into existence, it was spoken into existence by Jesus (The Word of God). The Spirit of the Father is what manifested what was spoken by Jesus (The Word of God). **If the Devil can convince man that he doesn't exist, he can convince man that God doesn't exist, because Father God created Lucifer/Satan/The Devil.**

**Revelation 4:2-3** says, "And immediately I was in the spirit: and, behold, a throne was set in heaven, and one sat on the throne. And he that sat was to look upon like a **jasper** and a **sardine** stone: and there was a rainbow round about the throne, in sight like unto an emerald." **(The Father looked like a precious stone. Precious stones shine, reflect light, colors, and are long-lasting. Precious stones on Earth symbolize the precious stones in Heaven. Precious metals like gold are related to their prototype in Heaven as well. Our DNA is of crystal.)**

**Revelation 1:14 -15** says, "His head and his hairs were white like wool, as white as snow; and his eyes were as a flame of fire; And his feet like unto fine brass, as if they burned in a furnace; and his voice as the sound of many waters." **(The sun shines as a white light up top, and the earth's rich soil is black on the bottom (from head to feet). His head was white and his feet are brass brown to black, which represents the lack of color to the abundance of color. Each end of the color spectrum. Every color is in between white and black. The clouds are white like wool and the blue sky symbolizes a blue flame. The sun symbolizes a red flame. The rainbow, blue sky, and red sun symbolizes every eye color white people have. His feet as brass burned in a furnace symbolizes black and brown such as melanated people. When Black people birth an albino, although the skin of the child is white, its hair remains wooly.**

***Heritage (definition): something that is or may be inherited; property passing at the owner's death to the heir or those entitled to succeed; legacy.**

***Portion (def.); birthright; heritage: "Absolute rule was considered the inheritance of kings."**

***Begotten (def.); to father; to cause or create.**

**Hebrews 1:2-9** says, "Hath in these last days spoken unto us by his Son, **whom he hath appointed heir of all things, by whom also he made the worlds;**

3 Who being the brightness of his glory, and the express image of his person, and upholding all things by the word of his power, when he had by himself purged our sins, **sat down on the right hand of the Majesty on high:**

4 **Being made so much better than the angels**, as he hath **by inheritance** obtained a more excellent name than they.

5 For unto which of the angels said he at any time, Thou art my Son, **this day have I begotten thee**? And again, **I will be to him a Father, and he shall be to me a Son?**

6 And again, when he bringeth in the firstbegotten into the world, he saith, And let all the angels of God worship him.

7 And of the angels he saith, Who maketh his angels spirits, and his ministers a flame of fire.

8 But unto the Son he saith, Thy throne, O God, is for ever and ever: **a sceptre of righteousness is the sceptre of thy kingdom.**

9 **Thou hast loved righteousness, and hated iniquity; therefore God, even thy God, hath anointed thee with the oil of gladness above thy fellows.**"

Jesus was made so much better than the angels. He inherited a more excellent name, and the angels of the Father God were led to worship him. God established his throne forever, and a scepter of righteousness is the scepter of his kingdom. Jesus loved righteousness, and hated iniquity so he is anointed above all of his fellows. Iniquity was found in the Devil, Lucifer, or Satan, so he was cast out along with 1/3 of the angels that fell with him.

To mention **"this day have I begotten thee"** entails that before that day he was not exalted to the position he is now in. The only way to be transformed, exalted, and brought closer unto God is by the Spirit of God. Jesus (The

Word of God) had the spirit before he was exalted, but by the power of the Spirit, in which all things are made, he was made better. The Father and the spirit are one. The Father begat Jesus (The Word of God), and now the Father, Son, and the Holy Spirit are one. Now Jesus (The Word of God) is the heir of the Kingdom. Jesus became God after he was exalted to Godhood because he was given all power and authority.

**Jesus (The Word) was a creation in heaven that loved righteousness and hated iniquity more so than his fellows.***

Jesus is God because the father appointed Jesus (The word of God) heir of all things, by whom also he made the worlds. Therefore, if The Father God made the worlds by Jesus (The word of God), then Jesus (The word of God) is God over what was created. The Most High Father God gives his sons that are obedient inheritance over creation that is in their particular likeness. Jesus inherits (saints) men of righteousness. The faith of Abraham is what made him the father of the Hebrew Israelite heritage. In order to be brought into Jesus as the Bride of Christ, we must follow the way of Jesus Christ, by faith, and love righteousness. We have to die daily in order to stay born again after we receive the gift of the Holy Spirit. **Children of God have free will so Jesus Christ accepted his death before earth was created. God's plan was already established before the creation of earth began.**

**Revelation 13:8** says, "And all that dwell upon the earth shall worship him, whose names are not written in the book of life of the **Lamb slain from the foundation of the world.**"

***Jesus had to pray, fast, be obedient, suffer and die. God ordained us to be like Christ. So it's God's will, we have to pray, fast, be obedient, suffer (deny self of worldly pleasures), accept execution, or survive until he comes back to bring down New Jerusalem. Then after one thousand years we enter into the final Judgement and go to Heaven and get our position according to our works on earth.**

**John 1:18** says, "**No man hath seen God at any time, the only begotten Son, which is in the bosom of the Father, he hath declared him**."

**John 14:6** "I am the way, the truth, and the life: no man cometh unto the Father, but by me."

**John 6:57** "As the living Father hath sent me, and I live by the Father: so he that eateth me, even he shall live by me."

**Galatians 1:1** "Paul, an apostle, (not of men, neither by man, but by Jesus Christ, and God the Father, who raised him from the dead."

**Matthew 10:32** "Whosoever therefore shall confess me before men, him will I confess also before my Father which is in heaven."

**Matthew 7:21** "Not every one that saith unto me, Lord, Lord, shall enter into the kingdom of heaven; but he that doeth the will of my Father which is in heaven."

**Those of us that are saved by grace through the righteousness of Jesus (The Word of God) will be made better (born again as Jesus was, when he was begotten) to be joint heirs of the Kingdom of God with Jesus (The**

**Word of God). The process Jesus went through relates to the process we have to go through in order for us to be married as the Bride of Christ, or adopted into the Body of Christ. We can't obtain the righteousness of Jesus unless The Father sends the Holy Ghost to guide and convict us, so we have to believe in Jesus Christ for him to send the Holy Ghost of the Father (The Comforter) to us.**

Jesus (The Word of God), spoke creation into existence. Jesus (The Word of God) spoke to Moses through the burning bush. All we have is our word, words are spirit, by our words we'll be justified and by our words we'll be condemned, and it's not what enters the mouth that defiles, but what comes out of the mouth. We was created by The Word, spoken into existence. **Our DNA is a Book of Life that consists of paragraphs, sentences, words, and letters. Our purpose, gifts, curses, traits, and everything about us is written in our DNA. That's why we have to be born again of the Spirit to get God DNA.** Not corruptible seed, but incorruptible seed. **Luke 8:11** says, "Now the parable is this: The seed is the word of God." We are born in sin, so we have to get the curse of the law removed from our genetics (biological book of life) by 'The Word of God.'

Everything God created with free will and consciousness to know good and evil is a son of God. One has to make a decision to love. Obedience to God is love, for God is love. Lucifer, or Satan was a disobedient son, and Jesus was obedient. Satan was punished, but Jesus was exalted. Our glory relies on our obedience. There are different species of conscious beings in Heaven. Jesus was chosen from among his particular species because of his righteousness. **The will of God exist on earth as it is in heaven. Employes that keep rules and regulations move up to managerial or leadership positions in every**

**establishment. However, it's not always about what you know, its who you know. If you don't know Jesus Christ, you're going to Hell.**

**Matthew 5:19** says, "Whosoever therefore shall break one of these least commandments, and shall teach men so, he shall be called the **least in the kingdom of heaven**: but whosoever shall do and teach them, the same shall be called **great in the kingdom of heaven.**"

**The species of angels that Jesus was created in, have the same form as man. The Father with his begotten son Jesus (The Word of God), created man in their image and likeness to have dominion over the earth.** God's will is for man to become transformed into the righteous image of his only begotten son (the only one of his species). We were created in the image and likeness of his kind to follow the example of Jesus through righteousness. Faith is accounted for righteousness. We are righteous by the righteousness of God and not of ourselves.

**Isaiah 64:6** says, "But we are all as an unclean thing, and all our righteousnesses are as filthy rags; and we all do fade as a leaf; and our iniquities, like the wind, have taken us away."

**John 1:1** says, "In the beginning was the Word, and the Word was with God, and the Word was God."

**Genesis 1:1** says, "In the beginning God created the heavens and the earth." **(The beginning is confirmed as the beginning of the world that was created, not the beginning of The Father for he is eternal).**

Man cannot be good without the power of the Holy Spirit because of our flesh. That's why "The Word" (Jesus) died for our sins as the last blood sacrifice, so that we may have a chance for salvation through belief in him. Jesus sends us the Holy Ghost to comfort us, lead us to all truth, help us endure till the end, and keep our DNA in the Book of Life. We have to be like Jesus and stand for righteousness like he did in order to be heirs of the kingdom with him. He came to show us how to be led by the Holy Ghost, teach, and endure till the end even through sufferings.

**John 15:13** says, "Greater love hath no man than this, that a man lay down his life for his friends." **(God is Love and he suffered in the flesh, became a curse for us by taking on the sins of the world and gave his life for all that whoever believes in him can be saved. He died for us so we can have life (now/eternal). To die for him would be gaining life.)**

**Matthew 10:39** says, "He that findeth his life shall lose it: and he that loseth his life for my sake shall find it."

Everything on earth is created in the image of something in Heaven. There are many different species in heaven as on Earth. **Earth is like a mirror of what's in heaven, but Heaven has much more glory like a mansion to a dog house.** Man was made in the image of Jesus (The Word of God). Man is the only creature that uses words and is exalted above every other creature. "The Word of God" is exalted above every other angel. The Devil or Satan was a son of God in heaven with free will like Jesus, but he chose iniquity over righteousness. One has to have the knowledge of good and evil to do evil. That's why the serpent deceived Eve to choose knowledge and intellect over obedience.

**Satan is classified as a dragon according to the Bible**. Birds of a feather flock together, so the angels that fell with him must have been reptilian. I believe that the dinosaurs were a species that were linked to the fallen angels by hybridization. Most of the fallen angels had to be reptilian, because God said he gave us power to tread over serpents, and serpents are reptiles and demons. If you look at all the pictures on the wall in the pyramids, you will see depictions of reptilian looking people that were either fallen angels and/or hybrids (giants born from fallen angels and human women). Every ancient culture has some dragon symbol, especially in Asia.

**Revelation 12:9** says, "And the great dragon was cast out, that old serpent, called the Devil, and Satan, which deceiveth the whole world: he was cast out into the earth, and his angels were cast out with him."

**All creation that our Father expects to be obedient to him are Sons of God. Moreover, those that are led by the spirit of God can call themselves the Sons of God. The Holy Spirit makes us sons of God.** We are children to whom we obey. The Holy Spirit helps us with obedience. The Devil did have a high position in heaven, beautiful with music embedded in him. He had pride, was envious of Jesus and the creation of man that was in the image and likeness of Jesus. The Devil and the rest of the fallen angels have only the power God allows them to have, and they use their power to kill, steal, and destroy. Jesus (The Word of God) came so that we may have life. It took him to lay down his life for us to have life. For God made laws upon creation of man, and one of the laws was there is no forgiveness of sin without the shedding of blood. Giving up a precious possession is a sacrifice. Killing a precious lamb reminds people that death is imminent, and seeing something die reminds us that we are flesh. Sheep represent humility and vulnerability. Sheep need a shepherd for protection, for they are helpless around predators (demons) without one. **The only protection and significance in us is the Holy Spirit. That reminder keeps us humble as sheep.**

**Ecclesiastes 7:2** says, "It is better to go to the house of mourning, than to go to the house of feasting: for that is the end of all men; and the living will lay it to his heart."

***Jesus is also called the 'Lamb of God', because he gave his life as the last blood sacrifice required to receive forgiveness of sin.***

**John 1:29** says, "The next day John seeth Jesus coming unto him, and saith, Behold the Lamb of God, which taketh away the sins of the world."

**Revelation 7:17** says, "For the Lamb which is in the midst of the throne shall feed them, and shall lead them unto living fountains of waters: and God shall wipe away all tears from their eyes."

**Revelation 22:3** says, "And there shall be no more curse: but the throne of God and of the Lamb shall be in it; and his servants shall serve him."

*****The Father and Son are one with the Holy Ghost the same way the water molecule is 3 in 1.** H2O; 2Hydrogen and 1 Oxygen. Fluid, ice, and steam, with steam and oxygen representing the Holy Ghost. The Holy Spirit is in all things keeping it alive the way oxygen is in all things keeping it alive. We can go days without food and water, but only minutes without oxygen. We can feel oxygen, but we can't see oxygen. We can feel the Holy Ghost, but we can't see the Holy Ghost. The Holy Ghost manifested what we do see, and oxygen keeps alive what we do see. We are all witnesses to the fact that what we don't see is more real than what we do see, because what we can't see created what we do see. **This is why blaspheming the Holy Ghost is an unforgivable sin.**

The Spirit of God is seen in the atom which is the building block of creation. You have to check out quantum physics for the details. The electron in the atom shows the characteristics of the Spirit, having the ability to jump from place to place without occupying the space in between. Photons, ions, and electron is said to have teleportation properties. When atoms are separated from its host and changed, the host can also be effected although they are not attached. This is why witches, by the way of voodoo, can take your hair or fingernails and put curses on you.

An atom is mostly empty space, but it's full of energy. Our bodies are actually empty space, but full of energy. The body is like an energy field interacting with many diverse energy fields in the atmosphere. Spirits are energy fields. This is how micro waves can travel through our bodies. This is how evil spirits can possess people and make them levitate, astral project, and take over the pineal gland and movements.

**Luke 12:10** says, "And whosoever shall speak a word against the Son of man, it shall be forgiven him: but unto him that blasphemeth against the Holy Ghost it shall not be forgiven."

***The Spirit of God is in all living things maintaining life, so when the spirit of God leaves, the host dies.***

**Genesis 25:8** says " Then Abraham gave up the ghost, and died in a good old age, an old man, and full of years; and was gathered to his people."

**Acts 12:23** says, "And immediately the angel of the Lord smote him, because he gave not God the glory: and he was eaten of worms, and gave up the ghost."

**All science does is try to figure out God's creation, but without the creator we will never understand the blueprint.**

**1 Corinthians 13:9 says,** "For we know in part, and we prophesy in part. Verse 12 says, "For now we see through a glass, darkly; but then face to face: now I know in part; but then shall I know, even as also I am known." **(Simply means that we see only what God allows us to see, and when we come into the presence of the Lord, our eyes will be open to see the fullness thereof.)**

**The eye actually follows the God ratio, or what we know as the Fibonacci sequence or spiral.** This is the ratio that a man by the name of Fibonacci realized was in all of creation, which is Gods pattern or signature in his creation. You can see the Fibonacci spiral or God's pattern when you look at the galaxy, a rams horn, a satellite image of a hurricane, a tornado, DNA, a fetus, an umbilical cord, the outer ear, the inner ear, the pineal gland, a sea shell, the way water swirls down a drain, a large wave in the ocean, or the way ripples in water expand when you throw something in a body of water like a pond. Everybody has the pattern on the top of their head, in the center of the hair, some call a 'cow lick.' When you roll up paper like a scroll, it still follows the spiral pattern. **Isaiah 34:4** and **Revelation 6:14**, in a time with no telescopes, talks about the heavens rolled together as a scroll. If you look at the picture of the galaxy, it is actually in the same pattern at the ends of paper rolled up as a scroll.

# THE LIKENESS AND IMAGE OF GOD

**Psalm 139:14 says, "I will praise thee; for I am fearfully and wonderfully made: marvellous are thy works; and that my soul knoweth right well."**

**Colossians 3:11** says, "Where there is neither Greek nor Jew, circumcision nor uncircumcision, Barbarian, Scythian, bond nor free: but Christ is all, and in all. "

**Colossians 1:16** says, "For by him were all things created, that are in heaven, and that are in earth, visible and invisible, whether they be thrones, or dominions, or principalities, or powers: all things were created by him, and for him.

**Revelation 4:11** says, "Thou art worthy, O Lord, to receive glory and honour and power: for thou hast created all things, and for thy pleasure they are and were created."

**2 Peter 3:5** says, "For this they willingly are ignorant of, that by the word of God the heavens were of old, and the earth standing out of the water and in the water."

**Genesis 1:26** says, "And God said, Let us make man in our image, after our likeness: and let them have dominion over the fish of the sea, and over the fowl of the air, and over the cattle, and over all the earth, and over every creeping thing that creepeth upon the earth."

**Blood has red blood cells and white blood cells. Blood also has platelets that make the blood clot up when we bleed. The red blood cells carry oxygen. The white**

**blood cells fight infection and anything that defiles the body. The platelets preserve life.**

**Isaiah 1:18** says, "Come now, and let us reason together, saith the Lord: though your sins be as scarlet, they shall be as white as snow; though they be red like crimson, they shall be as wool."

**Leviticus 17:11 says,** "For the life of the flesh is in the blood: and I have given it to you upon the altar to make an atonement for your souls: for it is the blood that maketh an atonement for the soul."

**Ephesians 1:7** says, "In whom we have redemption through his blood, the forgiveness of sins, according to the riches of his grace."

**The Father gave his son the souls of man as an inheritance. The son is to be married to those that believe. The body of Christ is the Bride of Christ.** The Bride of Christ are those that are saved to be joint heirs with Jesus Christ.

**We were created in God's image and likeness, so we have consciousness and have a way to relate with God. The pineal gland is in our brains, which we have to connect with the Holy Spirit.** The pineal gland is called the Spiritual Molecule. The pineal gland is where our dreams come from. We communicate with God via the pineal gland. God made us compatible with him so that we can communicate. Spiritual gifts in people are determined by the level their pineal gland is activated. The Spirit is what gives the pineal gland its power. We have consciousness, which is the primary attribute of God. Prayer and meditation exercises the pineal gland. Fasting and prayer stimulates the pineal gland and makes it easier for us to hear the voice of God.

We have to weaken the flesh to make room for the Spirit. If we meditate on anything else besides the Word of God, we can attract any other demonic spirit in the atmosphere. This is where the concept of the Law of Attraction comes from. Whatever you meditate on is what you draw to you. Our thoughts from our pineal gland bears witness to either the Holy Spirit or some other spirit.

God has not given us a spirit of fear but of power, love, and of a sound mind. Scary movies and the media specializes in imparting the spirit of fear on the population. The poisons in food and water is an attack on the pineal gland to make it hard to connect with God and make sound decisions. **God's word is spirit, so the more we read and meditate on his word, the more we draw the Holy Spirit and push out demonic spirits. The pineal gland is the heart of our mind that controls the heart of our body by the spirit of God that is electrical.**

***Proverbs 4:23** says, "Keep thy **heart (pineal gland)** with all diligence; for out of it are the issues of life."

**Hebrews 8:10** says, "For this is the covenant that I will make with the house of Israel after those days, saith the Lord**; I will put my laws into their mind, and write them in their hearts**: and I will be to them a God, and they shall be to me a people."

**The heavenly structure is symbolically ingrained into our genetics. The heart of the body symbolizes the throne of God. The heart consists of 4 chambers correlating with the 4 part cherubim where the throne of God sits.** The arc of the covenant was to be carried by four

Levite priest. The four cherubs where the throne of God sits are heavenly beasts. The arc of the covenant also symbolizes the pituitary gland and pineal gland.

**Revelation 4:6** says, "And before the throne there was a **sea of glass like unto crystal**: and in the midst of the throne, and round about the throne, were four beasts full of eyes before and behind." **Surrounding the human heart is a sack of water called the 'Pericardium.' The water of the pericardium is salt water like the sea of glass John saw in Revelation 4:6. DNA is of crystal.**

**Revelation 4:5** says, "And out of the throne proceeded lightnings and thunderings and voices, and there were seven lamps of fire burning before the throne, which are the seven Spirits of God." **A heart beat sounds like thunder, and electricity is what makes the heartbeat. Our voice comes from the air in our lungs. The lungs have seven vascular bundles representing the seven spirits of God.**

**Revelation 4:4** says, "And round about the throne were four and twenty seats: and upon the seats I saw four and twenty elders sitting, clothed in white raiment; and they had on their heads crowns of gold." **The white rib cage represents the 4 and 20 elders in white that surround the throne. The left side of our rib cage symbolizes the Old Testament and the right side the New Testament. The rib symbolizes completion. Eve was created from Adam's rib in which the woman completes the man.**

**The spine has 33 vertebra. Jesus was 33 years old when he was crucified.** When God came to Moses in **Exodus 33:23**, he said, "I will take away mine hand and thou shalt see my back parts; but my face shall not be seen." **God was revealing Jesus.** Jesus said, "If you have seen me, you have seen the father." The spine consist of 7 vertebrae in the cervical region, 12 in the thoracic region, 5 in the lumbar region, 5 in the sacral region, and 4 in the coccygeal region. Seven is the number of completion. Twelve disciples and twelve months in a year. Five fingers on the left hand represents the Father and Old Testament. Five fingers on the right hand represents Jesus and the New Testament. Jesus is referred to as the right hand. **Psalms 89:13** says, "Thou has a mighty arm: strong is thy hand, and high is thy right hand." **Our DNA has 4 base pairs (Adenine, Cytosine, Guanine, and Thymine) that connect the two strands of DNA together, and the four gospels connect the Old and New Testament. We also have four blood types which are A, B, AB and O.**

**The body is the temple of God. God told Solomon how to build the temple.** All of the stones of Solomon's temple may represent the many cells that make up the human body.

1 Peter 2:5 says, "Ye also, as lively stones, are built up a spiritual house, an holy priesthood, to offer up spiritual sacrifices, acceptable to God by Jesus Christ." **We are all the stones that make up the church. The word 'temple' is in the Bible 208 times, and it's said that we have 208 bones in our body.**

**Solomon's temple had the two pillars Jachin and Boaz that represents the two strands of DNA or chromosome pair in man. Each of the two pillars, Jachin and Boaz, in Solomon's temple, were 23 cubits tall that equal 46 cubits in all. In each cell of our bodies we have 23 pair of chromosomes that equal 46 in all.**

We all have **23** from our mother and **23** from our father. As in **Genesis 2:23-24**, a man and a woman come together as one flesh. This represents the **chromosomes from the mother** that come together with the **chromosomes of the father** that makes a **baby with 46 chromosomes.** In **Genesis 2:23-24**, the exact phrase that Adam said has **46 words.** In **1 Corinthians 3:16-17**, the **46 book in the bible**, has a phrase saying, **ye are the temple of God.' John 2:20-21** has the phrase **'Forty and six years was this temple in building, but he spoke of the temple of his body.'**

# DNA IS A BOOK OF LIFE

## (Genesis – Genes)

## (Within every seed is the DNA of its kind)

**Luke 8:11** says, "Now the parable is this: The seed is the word of God." **All seed has it's own DNA. All creation has seed. Everything was created by the word of God. Jesus is the word of God. Jesus is the seed. Jesus is the DNA we have to be born again into by the Holy Spirit.**

**Genesis 5:1** says, "This is the book of the generations of Adam. In the day that God created man, in the likeness of God made he him."

**Matthew 1:1** says, "The book of the generation of Jesus Christ, the son of David, the son of Abraham."

**Psalm 139:16** says, "Thine eyes did see my substance, yet being unperfect; and in thy book all my members were written, which in continuance were fashioned, when as yet there was none of them."

**Psalm 40:7-8** says, "Then said I, Lo, I come: in the volume of the book it is written of me, I delight to do thy will, O my God: yea, thy law is within my heart."

**Psalm 69:28** says, "Let them be blotted out of the book of the living, and not be written with the righteous."

**Hebrews 12:2** says, "Looking unto Jesus the *author* and finisher of our faith; who for the joy that was set before him endured the cross, despising the shame, and is set down at the right hand of the throne of God."

**1 Chronicles 9:1** says, "So all Israel were reckoned by genealogies; and, behold, they were written in the book of the kings of Israel and Judah, who were carried away to Babylon for their transgression."

**2 Chronicles 12:15** says, "Now the acts of Rehoboam, first and last, are they not written in the book of Shemaiah the prophet, and of Iddo the seer concerning genealogies? And there were wars between Rehoboam and Jeroboam continually."

**Exodus 32:32** says, "Yet now, if thou wilt forgive their sin--; and if not, blot me, I pray thee, out of thy book which thou hast written."

**Exodus 32:33** says, "And the Lord said unto Moses, Whosoever hath sinned against me, him will I blot out of my book."

**Hebrews 10:7** says, "Then said I, Lo, I come (in the volume of the book it is written of me,) to do thy will, O God."

**Revelation 3:5** says, "He that overcometh, the same shall be clothed in white raiment; and I will not blot out his name out of the book of life, but I will confess his name before my Father, and before his angels."

DNA has two strands that are connected by four base pairs. The four bases in DNA's alphabet are Adenine, Cytosine, Guanine, and Thymine. Adenine connects with Thymine, and Guanine connects with Cytosine that connect the two strands of DNA. **These four bases bring the two**

**strands of DNA together the way the 4 gospels of Matthew, Mark, Luke, and John bring the Old and the New Testament together.**

When the base pairs, Adenine, Cytosine, Guanine, and Thymine connect with their designated pair, they form genes. Each gene is in a sequence that stops as if it has a period at the end of the sequence. **They have found out that DNA can be read like a book.** When the base pairs connect, they form amino acids. By the way of the base pairs, the amino acids are what forms the genes. There are 22 amino acids that make the genes, which form the letters, and make the words that form the book of our DNA.

**The 22 amino acids are in correlation with the 22 letters of the Hebrew alphabet of which Old Testament was written. The New Testament was written in Greek, which has 24 letters. 22+24=46, which represents the 46 chromosomes that contain the book of our DNA. Letters form words, and words form books. DNA form chromosomes, and chromosomes form cells.**

***Generation means genes***

**Genesis 5:1** says "This is the book of the generations of Adam.

**Matthew 1:1** says "The book of the generation of Jesus Christ.. **(The book of their genes. The book is DNA.)**

**Psalm 139:16** says, "Thine eyes did see my substance, yet being imperfect; and in thy book all my members were written, which in continuance were fashioned, when as yet there was none of them." **(David is**

**saying that all his members were written in his book of DNA before he was born.)**

**Isaiah 34:16** says, "Seek ye out of the book of the Lord, and read: not one of these shall fail, none shall want her mate: for my mouth it hath commanded, and his spirit it hath gathered them." **(None shall want her mate correlates to the base pairs that connect the two strands of DNA, and how every scripture in the Old Testament has a mate in the New Testament that's connected by the four gospels. Spiritual things are confirmed by spiritual things. Adenine and Guanine are confirmed by Cytosine and Thymine. The Old Testament is confirmed by the New Testament. However, Gods' spirit has gathered them.)**

**The tabernacle that Moses built is a representation of each individual cell in our body.** It has 20 boards on each side with 6 boards on the back, which represents the 46 chromosomes that's within each cell. Four boards were put on the front of the tabernacle that represents the four base pairs or the four gospels.

In the tabernacle 23,000 priest were to perform sacrifices at the altar.. The two types of sacrifices that were acceptable were meat or grain. The sacrifices were to be prepared and burned on the altar before the Lord. Our cells go through the same process. We prepare our food. When we eat meat or grain, the content of our food is distributed to the cells. The altar is the nucleus of the cell. The cells burn up the nutrients, which converts into sugar, and the sugar gives energy to the cell, allowing our cells to reproduce. We tend to eat every day. God told us in his word what to eat and what is unclean to eat. We are what we eat. **Our cells represent a continuous sacrifice.**

**Romans 12:1** says, "I beseech you therefore, brethren, by the mercies of God, that ye present your bodies a living sacrifice, holy, acceptable unto God, which is your reasonable service." **(Our cells symbolize the sacrifices of the temple, and we are to sacrifice our flesh to be led by the spirit.)**

**The word sacrifice is used in 23 verses in the New Testament. 23+23=46, but representing being born again with God DNA.** In **Romans 1:29-31, there is exactly 23 sins we need a sacrifice for.**

**Romans 3:23** says, "For all have sinned, and come short of the glory of God."

**Romans 6:23** says, "For the wages of sin is death, but the gift of God is eternal life through Jesus Christ our Lord."

**It was 46 words the serpent in the garden spoke to Eve to get her to eat from the Tree of Knowledge of Good and Evil. We all inherit the sins of our parents. Therefore, we are all born sinners, so we have to be born again to enter into the kingdom of God.**

**1 Peter 1:23** says, "Being born again, not of corruptible seed, but of incorruptible, by the word of God, which liveth and abideth for ever." Adam was corruptible seed, but Jesus is incorruptible seed. **If we are only born once, we die twice. The lake of fire is the second death. If we're born twice, we die once.** Being born again is receiving the Holy Ghost and being transformed by the renewing of the mind. What's impossible for man is highly possible for God.

**Revelation 20:14** says "And death and hell were cast into the lake of fire. This is the second death."

**Matthew 7:19** says, "Every tree that bringeth not forth good fruit is hewn down, and cast into the fire."

**Colossians 2:13-14** says, "And you, being dead in your sins and the uncircumcision of your flesh, hath he quickened together with him, having forgiven you all trespasses; **Blotting out the handwriting of ordinances** that was against us, which was contrary to us, and took it out of the way, nailing it to his cross." **(In the 23 book of the Bible, Isaiah 53:4-5, told everything Christ did as a sacrifice for us on the cross. In the 46 book of the New Testament, Luke 2:10-11, an angel declared the birth of Jesus. The chromosomes, in our cells, look like crosses the way they connect with each other.)**

**Galatians 2:20** says, "I am crucified with Christ: nevertheless I live; yet not I, but Christ liveth in me."

***The image of DNA looks like a winding ladder.***

**Genesis 28:12** says, "And he dreamed, and behold a ladder set up on the earth, and the top of it reached to heaven: and behold the angels of God ascending and descending on it."

**John 1:51** says, "And he saith unto him, Verily, verily, I say unto you, Hereafter ye shall see heaven open, and the angels of God ascending and descending upon the Son of man." **This is an example of the Old and New Testament scripture confirming one another. Jesus is the ladder the angels ascend and descend upon. The ladder symbolizes DNA. DNA looks like a ladder. DNA represents life. Jesus (The Word of God) spoke life into**

**existence. Jesus is life. The angels only can exist in the life Jesus provides for them. The angels can only ascend and descend upon the ladder of life provided, which Jesus (The Word of God) is responsible for.**

***Solomon's temple has another symbol of DNA.***

**1 Kings 6:8** says, "The door for the middle chamber was in the right side of the house: and they went up with winding stairs into the middle chamber, and out of the middle into the third." (From the lower level of the temple to the upper level of the temple, **Solomon built a spiral staircase, which is exactly the picture of DNA.)**

**In one helical turn of DNA, there are 10 nucleotides that connect the two strands, which look like stairs. The word stairs is written in the Bible 10 times. The Ten Commandments were written on two tablets of stone, and DNA is a crystal, literally like two stones side by side.**

**Romans 2:15** says, "Which shew the work of the law written in their hearts, their conscience also bearing witness, and their thoughts the mean while accusing or else excusing one another." **(The law is written in our hearts.** If we listen to our heart, we already know right from wrong. Our thoughts are the deceitful, compromising vehicle of disobedience.)

**2 Corinthians 3:3** says, "Forasmuch as ye are manifestly declared to be the epistle of Christ ministered by us, written not with ink, but with the Spirit of the living God; not in tables of stone, but in fleshy tables of the heart."

**Luke 4:4** says, "And Jesus answered him, saying, it is written, that man shall not live by bread alone, but by every word of God." **(The word of God in the Bible, and the word of God written in our DNA.)**

**We inherit the sin and curse of our parents in our DNA, and that's why we have to be born again by the Holy Spirit.** Sin corrupts DNA. When we are born again, God cleanses the curse from our genetics; for man shall not live by bread alone, but by every word written in the Bible and in our DNA.

**Acts 12:24** says, "But the word of God grew and multiplied." **(The cells that make up our body, grow and multiply. The cells in our body contain DNA, the book of life that grow and multiply.)**

**DNA is God's book that is not to be tampered with. That's why God said don't add or take away from my book. We are not supposed to add or take away from DNA. DNA is God's book that he wrote. The author and finisher of our faith. We are ordained through DNA (The book of our life that God wrote).**

**Genesis 5:1** says "This is the book of the generations of Adam."

**Matthew 1:1** says "The book of the generation of Jesus Christ." **(Generation means genes. The book of his genes, referring to the genes of his for-fathers (David etc.) that contributed to his genetics.)**

**Psalms 69:28** says, "Let them be blotted out of the book of the living…"

**Philippians 4:3** says, "…whose names are in the book of life." (The Bible is life, and life is literally anything that has a book of DNA. **The Bible tells us who**

**we are, and why we are here. Our DNA holds all the words (genetics) of who we are. When our DNA is corrupted by demonic possession, we are outside the book of Life.)**

***Like I stated earlier, everything on earth has a correlation in heaven. DNA is linked to the Book of Life in Heaven.***

Now DNA has 2 strands. We have the first Adam, and the second Adam (which is Jesus), Old Testament and the New Testament, Law and Grace, Ishmael and Isaac, Jacob and Esau, Old Jerusalem and New Jerusalem, Slavery in Egypt and Slavery in America. **America is the spiritual Egypt. It's a place of bondage, slavery, and it's deceitfully demonic.** We have a left lung and right lung, left eye and right eye, left ear and right ear, left hand and right hand, Jesus Christ is at the Father's right hand, and the New Testament is on the right side of the Bible. **The right hand has 27 bones, and the New Testament has 27 books.**

**Numbers 10:2** says,...make thee two trumpets of silver for the calling of the assembly."

**Psalms 12:6** says, "The words of the LORD are pure words: as silver tried in a furnace of earth, purified seven times." **(Old and New Testament correlating with the two trumpets of silver in Numbers 10:2.)**

**Revelation 1:10** says, "I was in the Spirit on the Lord's day, and heard behind me a great voice, as of a trumpet." **(The ear to hear follows the Fibonacci or God's pattern, and the ram's horn used as a trumpet, which sounds like the voice of Jesus, follows the same pattern.)**

Man was created in God's likeness and image (meaning compatible DNA). This is how Jesus, which is, "The Word," was able to be manifested, by the spirit, through a woman. This is how Jesus could be God and man at the same time, because our DNA is compatible with God's DNA, which was made possible by the Spirit in which all things are made.

***For the invisible things of God, from the creation of the world, are clearly seen, being understood by the things that are made, even his eternal power and Godhead, so that we are without excuse.***

# THE FALLEN ANGELS CORRUPT DNA

**Enoch 7:1-2 & 9-15** says, "It happened after the sons of men had multiplied in those days, that daughters were born to them, elegant and beautiful.

2. And when the angels, the sons of heaven, beheld them, they became enamoured of them, saying to each other, Come, let us select for ourselves wives fron the progeny of men, and let us beget children.

9. These are the names of their chiefs: Aamyaza, who was their leader, Urakabarameel, Akibeel, Tamiel, Ramuel, Danel, Azkeel, Saraknyal, asael, Armers, Batraal, Anane, Zavebe, Samsaveel, Ertael, Turel, Yomyael, and Arazyal. These were the perfects of the two hundred angels, and the remainder were all with them.

10. Then they took wives, each choosing for himself; whom they began to approach, and with whom they cohabited; teaching them sorcery, incantations, and the diiding of roots and trees.

11. And the women conceiving brought forth giants.

12. Whose stature was each three hundred cubits. These devoured all which the labour of men produced; until it became impossible to feed them;

13. When they turned themseles against men, in order to devour them.

14. And began to inure birds, beast, reptiles, and fishes, to eat their flesh on after another, and to drink their blood.

15. Then the earth reproved the unrighteous.

**Enoch 8:1-9** says, "Moreoer Azazyel taught men to make swords, knives, shields, breastplates, the fabrication of mirrors, and the workmanship of bracelets and ornaments, the use of paint the beautifying of the eyebrows, the use of stones of every valuable and select kind, and of all sorts of dyes, so that the world became altered.

2. Impiety increased; fornication multiplied; adn they transgressed and corrupted all their ways.

3. Amazarak taught all the sorcerers, and dividers of roots:

4. Armers taught the solution of sorcery;

5. Barkayal taught the observers of the stars;

6. Akibeel taught signs;

7. Tamiel taught astronomy;

8. And Asaradel taught the motion of the moon.

9. And men, being destroyed, cried out; and their voice reached to heaven.

***ITS TIME FOR ALL MEN TO CRY OUT TO GOD***

**Matthew 24:37** says, **"But as the days of Noah were, so shall also the coming of the Son of man be."**

**Matthew 15:11** says, "Not that which goeth into the mouth defileth a man; but that which cometh out of the mouth, this defileth a man."

**Revelation 21:27** says, "And there shall in no wise enter into it anything that defileth, neither whatsoever worketh abomination, or maketh a lie: but they which are written in the Lamb's book of life."

**The reason for the flood of Noah was to wash out the corrupt DNA the Fallen Angels or Nephilim created by having offspring with human woman; furthermore, genetically modifying organisms with plants and animals the way they are doing today. The Devil wants to imitate God and take over God's creation. He wishes to control, genetically engineer, see and know everything by the way of technology. The Devil uses technology to make it like it was in the days of Noah. The Devil doesn't create, all he can do is pervert what God has already created. He doesn't have the power to see and know everything, so he uses surveillance and technology to store information. Only difference is he can't do it himself anymore, he has to use man to do it. The spirits of the hybrids stayed around to be the demonic force on earth in place of the fallen angels that are chained in darkness.**

The fallen angels always made underground tunnels, away of transportation, and more advanced technology than we are exposed to today. They are the ones who built the pyramids. Their hybrid children had smaller pyramids built. Most were for human sacrifices, landmarks according to ley lines and energy fields, rituals, and whatever purpose associated with demonic interest. The pictures in the

Egyptian pyramids depict hybrid beings of animal and human genetics. The Sphinx in Egypt is a depiction of a hybrid (part angelic and part man, for all animals are in the image of a particular species of angel in Heaven). They circumnavigated the globe when the earth was one land mass and after when the earth was divided.

**Genesis 10:25** says, "And unto Eber were born two sons: the name of one was Peleg; for in his days **was the earth divided....**"

**Ecclesiastes 1:9** says, "The thing that hath been, it is that which shall be; and that which is done is that which shall be done: and there is no new thing under the sun."

**The children of the fallen angels, which were the hybrids or giants that died in the flood. Most of them that lived in water remained. After the flood more giants were created.**

**Genesis 6:4** says, "There were giants in the earth in those days; **and also after that**."

**Those that remained after the flood continued the bloodline of the fallen angels (demons). These ancient bloodlines are those who the fallen angels communicate their secret agenda to.** These people were rulers of all the ancient empires. Today they are people that practice incest in order to keep the bloodline from being diluted. The Royal families of Europe ( The Monarcy), some of our presidents, some renowned philosophers, and people you wouldn't believe belong to these ancient, royal, demonic bloodlines.

**Every King has had to answer to, or be a servant to the priesthood of demons that hide behind the scenes.** The Pharaohs of Egypt are a good example of that. They also had to go through a ritual to channel a demon that would give them the right to rule. These are the same rituals that go on in today's society but in a more sophisticated form.

**The Devil needs representatives that the people will hearken to or be hypnotized by.** The 'White Brotherhood' is actually the demons that are the rulers of the darkness. The 'Red Brotherhood' is the white men that are in the bloodline that are the tools for the Devil's agenda. The globalists are all tools for the devil's agenda. The agenda is total control, and this can't happen without controlling all the natural resources of the world. **The Devil's agenda is to incorporate as much sin and fear necessary to make demonic possession an easier process for people to submit/bow to Satan and accept damnation before Jesus comes back.**

**When the hybrids or giants died in the flood, their spirits remained on Earth. The spirits of the giants are the evil spirits that torment and possess people every day.** The fallen angels are eternal and are doomed to hell. The fallen angels are locked away in the bottomless pit, a dimension in earth until they are released for judgement.

The way God judges the earth is by letting demons cause terrorism. The devil is trying to increase sin as much as possible so the fallen angels can have an abundance of people to possess and destroy when they are released. The zombie apocalypse is nothing but a multitude of demon possessed prone individuals. There are dimensional portals created by sin that demons can come through. The demons live in darkness. When we sin we collect darkness allowing demons to inhabit the darkness.

**Luke 11:34** says, "The light of the body is the eye: therefore when thine eye is single, thy whole body also is full of light; but when thine eye is evil, thy body also is full of darkness."

The hadron collider at Cern, Switzerland is fulfilling the book of revelation prophecy by collecting dark matter. Demons and fallen angels live in the darkness (abyss dimension), but humans exist in the light deminsion. Man receives darkness through sin, so thats why people can become possessed by demons by collecting darkness. The fallen angels are bound in chains in a dark dimension in the earth. **The fallen angels were the angels that were expelled from heaven along with Lucifer for rebelling against God. Lucifer (Satan) is trying to deceive people into thinking that the fallen angels are aliens.**

The giants or fallen angels, made people sacrifice their children. They also started cannibalism, because they ate the children. Vampires symbolize demons. Eating and drinking blood is demonic. God said not to eat blood because life is in the blood, parasites, disease and so forth. Blood is also spiritual. **Caucasians take pride in eating bloody meat. Rare, medium rare, medium, and medium well steaks have desensitized people to the concept of eating blood.**

**Proverbs 3:31** says, “Envy not the oppressor and choose none of his ways.”

*The Devil communicates his agenda to people that are within the ancient bloodlines of the fallen angels (spiritual wickedness in high places, and rulers of the darkness). These people are demonic in nature, and do not have natural compassion for human life. They feed off power, control, fear, death, and destruction. **Look up the ancient bloodline conspiracy**. Some people initiate into the bloodline by selling their soul and allowing themselves to be taken over by conjuring. Some people are taken and infused with a third strand of DNA. The modern knowledge of this is revealed through the **MK Ultra mind control program. The only thing that can repair DNA is the Holy Spirit.**

**Judges 21:10** says, "And the congregation sent thither twelve thousand men of the valiantest, and commanded them, saying, Go and smite the inhabitants of Jabeshgilead with the edge of the sword, with the women and the children." **(The reason why they were to kill women and children is because they were hybrid giants. They were not human.)**

The devil wants people to think that aliens put us here and they are coming back to save the Earth. That's all a part of the Great Deception. In reality, what they are calling aliens are the fallen angels and they've always been here. **The greatest trick the devil has pulled was to convince man that he wasn't real. If he can make man believe he's not real, he can convince man that God isn't real, because God created the devil.** The devil has been a liar and a murderer since the beginning. The fallen angels lost their first estate as angels and are now demons. **The demons can only opperate by law. God allows them to operate within the bounds of what he allows according to his will.**

**Doors open for demons to corrupt the Earth through demonic sacrifices, rituals, and sin. Demons feed off fear, horror, terror, pain, suffering, and stress. This is why we have the War on Terror, because it keeps people in a constant state of fear.**

**Many secret societies, have demonic rituals. 'Crossing the Burning Sands', is a demonic ritual in Greek fraternities and sororities.** They call it 'Hell Week'. Crossing the Burning Sands is what the Knights Templar called their journey back home after their defeat with the muslim army for trying to take over the land of Jerusalem. The Knights Templar were wicked. They made human sacrifices with baby boys. They would rape them, kill them, eat their flesh, and drink their blood. They collected the remains such as the genitals and the bones. This is where the skull and crossbones come from.

This is why most fraternities and sororities have initiations that involve some form of fear and pain involved. It falls in line with trauma based mind control. Fraternities are the training grounds for secret societies, because people in fraternities are trained to keep secrets. Fraternities do rituals, and a ritual is the way demons are conjured up. This is the reason why most of our leaders are not allowed to realy make a difference in our neighborhoods. The Boule is the perfect example of prestigious black leaders that just tell us to vote as the only solution.

Demonic possession corrupts the DNA of man, while the Holy Spirit restores DNA. When the DNA of God's creation becomes overwhelmingly corrupted, then it will be like it was in the days of Noah.

**Matthew 24:37** says, "But as the days of Noah were, so shall also the coming of the Son of man be."

**The fallen angels are those who are imparting all the technology to man in order to make Earth like it was in the days of Noah. Before the flood, there was technology on earth as well.**

1 **Peter 3:20** says, "Which sometime were disobedient, when once the longsuffering of God waited in the days of Noah, while the ark was a preparing, wherein few, that is, eight souls were saved by water."

**Matthew 7:14** says, "Because strait is the gate, and narrow is the way, which leadeth unto life, and few there be that find it."

**The Mark of the Beast is the chip technology that will test who can find the narrow way. The Mark of the Beast will permanently defile the DNA in man.** The mark will be the only way to buy or sell, therefore, many people will give in to it. The 'Mark' will reveal who is on God's side, and who isn't. **The Devil has a mark, but God has a seal.**

**Revelation 13:17** says, "And that no man might buy or sell, save he that had the mark, or the name of the beast, or the number of his name."

**Revelation 7:3** says, "Saying, Hurt not the earth, neither the sea, nor the trees, till we have sealed the servants of our God in their foreheads."

**Jeremiah 6:16** says, "Thus saith the Lord, Stand ye in the ways, and see, and ask for the old paths, where is the good way, and walk therein, and ye shall find rest for your souls." But they said, we will not walk therein." **(Relying on all this new technology and genetically modified food for your only hope will lead to defilled DNA.)**

**1 Timothy 6:20** says, "O Timothy, keep that which is committed to thy trust, avoiding profane and vain babblings, and oppositions of science falsely so called. Which some professing have erred concerning the faith."

**Matthew 13:24-30** says, "Another parable put he forth unto them, saying, The kingdom of heaven is likened unto a man which sowed good seed in his field:

25. But while men slept, his enemy came and sowed tares among the wheat, and went his way.

26. But when the blade was sprung up, and brought forth fruit, then appeared the tares also.

27. So the servants of the householder came and said unto him, Sir, didst not thou sow good seed in thy field? from whence then hath it tares?

28. He said unto them, An enemy hath done this. The servants said unto him, Wilt thou then that we go and gather them up?

29. But he said, Nay; lest while ye gather up the tares, ye root up also the wheat with them.

30. Let both grow together until the harvest: and in the time of harvest I will say to the reapers, Gather ye together first the tares, and bind them in bundles to burn them: but gather the wheat into my barn."

(If you can't walk with God now, it will be hard to walk with God then. Good men are surrounded by evil men. Right now the tares are growing with the wheat. When the wheat is ready for harvest, then it will be easy to distinguish between the two. **(Those who have the Holy Ghost and resist the Mark of the Beast will be saved like Noah and his family.)**

**We can use technology for good by spreading the truth. The Devil uses technology to convince man that they can become gods without the almighty God, which started with Eve and the serpent in the garden.** Before disobedience, Adam and Eve already had eternal life without any pain and suffering. All the pain and suffering came when men were influenced by the fallen angels to disobey God.

**The ancient hope is that man can live forever, with the help of technology, which is the driving force of the powers that be.** Satan has promised certain people (rulers of darkness and spiritual wickedness in high places) that they will live forever if they help him rule the world. Promising them they will be able to travel through galaxies and become gods themselves. He wants man to make space ships to escape earth before Jesus comes back. The purpose of going into outer space is to escape the Judgement of God. Satan knows he has no where to hide, but he has done a good job convincing certain people that they can. God knows and can see everything, so the Devil wants to know and see everything by using technology. The Devil wants to be in control and copy-cat everything God can do. That's the reason for all of this surveillance. **I believe the reason for atom bombs is to have some fire power to fight Jesus when he comes back, because Jesus is coming back to destroy the wicked and exalt those that belong to him for one thousand years until the final judgement in Revelation 20.**

**With technology, man can somewhat control the possession process in a way to fulfill the agenda of the Devil.** They are trying to add a third strand of DNA to everything. Mk Ultra Mind Control, Monsanto, and Project Blue Beam are examples of Satan's devices. Demonic possession can add and take away from DNA. They have created demonically controlled super soldiers that the powers that be are incrementally releasing to terrorize the earth. **Most terroristic activity is staged, false flag, Hegelian Dialectic (problem – reaction – solution). REPENT * REPENT * REPENT.**

Demonic possession corrupts man's DNA, that's why we have to be born again by the Holy Spirit and get God DNA through Jesus. Born again of the Second Adam. Not corruptible seed, but incorruptible seed. Being born again by the Holy Ghost is incorruptible. The Holy Spirit protects our DNA from being corrupted. Through Jesus we have the power to tread over serpents, for serpents are demons. **What's impossible for man is highly possible for God. It takes spirit to fight spirit, and we don't wrestle with flesh and blood, but against powers, principalities, spiritual wickedness in high places, and the rulers of the darkness of this age. We can't see what is attacking us, but the Holy Spirit by angels protect us from all that attacks us.**

The fallen angels taught men enchantments, sorcery, soothsaying, and several forms of witchcraft. They taught man how to make weapons and go to war, how to make dyes and ways for women to adorn themselves and paint their eyes. They also knew about astrology, energy fields, dimensions, ley lines, and the natural healing properties of the Earth.

Today as a tradition, some use herbs in voodoo witchcraft for the healing properties. There is a practice in voodoo called shifting. The witch doctor can use powers to shift a disease or illness from one part of the body to the other, without the power to heal, but to keep you coming back. **Pharmaceutical medicine is witchcraft. It helps the symptoms in one area while causing a host of problems in another. Pharmakeia is the Greek word for the use of drugs or medicines, sorcery, and witchcraft. Pharma is pharmakeia.**

The dynamic in which demons operate is in socrecy and deceit. They operate in darkness. The Most High God reveals mysteries, brings the truth to the light, and wants us to know how to receive life. Demons want to hide mysteries and keep us from life. **The Devil's only plan is to deceive us into believing light is dark, up is down, death is life, and wrong is right. The way of deception is by using what God already created, then figuring out how evil can get the glory for it.** The only way this unrighteous transition of perception can occur is by distorting knowledge.

For example: Monkeys (primates) resemble man because symbolism and correlation is in all of God's creation. Monkeys (primates) show man what to eat (fruit and herbs), and that man correlate with trees. **Matthew 12:33** says "Either make the tree good, and his fruit good; or else make the tree corrupt, and his fruit corrupt: for the tree is known by his fruit. Monkeys communicate with more conscious intelligence than any other animal. However, the Devil doesn't want us to have the knowledge of God. The Devil wants us to believe we evolved from monkeys.

**Another example is "Casper the friendly Ghost." The only friendly ghost is the Holy Ghost, and every other spirit is an evil spirit**. Then hollywood broadcast "Ghost Busters", as if they are who you suppose to call when something is strange in the neighborhood. The only power that can defeat an evil spirit is the angels of the most high God by the Holy Spirit in the name of Jesus Christ. That is just a few examples of deceit out of a multitude.

**Masons adhere to deception at its finest.** The pyramid is also the model in which the Devil operates. The top of the pyramid represents the chosen few who hold the critical knowledge. The bottom of the pyramid represents the mass of people who are ignorant of what the people at the top know. The pyramid structure has made its way into every aspect of our society. The system of the pyramid is to maintain slavery by keeping people ignorant of the knowledge of the next level.

Every company and corporation adheres to this system directly or indirectly. In order to graduate to the next level of privilege, you have to obtain the qualifications necessary to deserve the advancement. On the lower levels, one has to prove his efficiency and ability to take orders. On the higher levels, which some are inherently born into, one has to eventually pledge their allegiance to Lucifer. They never tell you what God they want you to pledge your allegiance to. They give you books with the Luciferian doctrine and expect you to figure it out. They just take you through rituals and ask you to spit on the cross. If you refuse, they know that you're not ready yet. They would eventually ask you who your god is, and if you don't say Lucifer then they know that you're not ready yet. They always play it off so that you continue to believe they are a Christian organization.

As long as you continue to believe that being a Mason is a righteous fraternity that's out for the good of mankind, then you'll never advance to the higher levels. This is how they keep power in the hands of people who serve the Devil. The people in the fraternity that do not serve the Devil are excluded from the higher circles and are used as pawns and servants in the community. The Devil always needs a pretty face to hide behind, so people don't see the ugly.

All knowledge comes from God. The Devil's knowledge is deceit. **He want's people to desire his hidden knowledge, which is this: "Through intellect, enlightenment, and technology, man can someday obtain godhood and live forever.** Demons gave man technology before the flood and demons gave man technology after the flood. This time man has to be the face so we don't figure out that evil is behind computers, Nasa, and the military industrial complex. God can use anything for good. The Devil comes to kill, steal, and destroy. Bombs do nothing but kill and destroy. War does nothing but creates an opportunity to steal resources by killing the people who own the land. The resources are used for artificial intelligence and the hydran collider at Cern. NASA was formed to escape the judgment of God that is coming upon the Earth. The planets are named after fallen angels, and who knows the truth about outer space when all we have is their word for it. **The book of Enoch informs us of Gods creation including the stars. I believe that planets are used as dog houses for angels that get kicked out of Heaven, and the protagonist unites with the Father to create beings to be tested by the antagonist for the inheritance of those that are faithful and believe in the righteousness of God.**

**Alien abductions are actually demon possession, and Nasa knows that the experience can be stopped by calling on Jesus.** They don't want people to know because that will expose the alien deception. They have just enough advanced technology to convince people that obtaining Godhood is possible. Transhumanism is not just a movement, it's been the devil's plan since the beginning. All he wants to do is add and take away from God's book of life (DNA), and add a third strand of demonic possession, which is perpetuated by technology.

Falling angels had knowledge of astronomy. Whatever is going on in the heavens is God's business. **God gave us his word and the whole of the matter is to fear God and keep his commandments.** Some of Gods ways are correlated to the heavens. The Devil tries to prove the word of God wrong by pointing out the correlation between the stars and events in the Bible. This is why God said it's not necessary to be an observer of times.

**Deuteronomy 18:10-14** says, "There shall not be found among you any one that maketh his son or his daughter to pass through the fire (child sacrifice/abortion), or that useth divination, or an observer of times, or an enchanter, or a witch.

11. Or a charmer, or a consulter with familiar spirits, or a wizard, or a necromancer.

12. For all that do these things are an abomination unto the LORD: and because of these abominations the LORD thy God doth drive them out from before thee.

13. Thou shalt be perfect with the LORD thy God.

**Isaiah 13:10** says, "For the stars of heaven and the constellations thereof shall not give their light: the sun shall be darkened in his going forth, and the moon shall not cause her light to shine."

**Psalm 8:3** says, "When I consider thy heavens, the work of thy fingers, the moon and the stars, which thou hast ordained."

**Job 25:5** says, "Behold even to the moon, and it shineth not; yea, the stars are not pure in his sight."

**Deuteronomy 18:14** says "For these nations, which thou shalt possess, hearkened unto observers of times, and unto diviners: but as for thee, the Lord thy God hath not suffered thee so to do." **(The reason why Joshua was ordered by God to kill everyone on the land they went to possess, was because the children of the fallen angels**

**were on the land. David and Goliath is an event where David slew a giant that was a descendant of a fallen angel. David's army went to war with many armies of hybrids.)**

There is word that something is moving towards Earth, and it's said that the Lucifer telescope with its inferred technology is the only way to see it being monitored from Mt. Graham. The Vatican is paving the way for an imminent alien savior, and is trying to make the timing and destination acceptable. This will be the great deception. Christianity will be radically reinterpreted, and people will be deceived into a demonic doctrine. The Anti-Christ will be a hybrid with demonic powers. He will be a worshiper of the fallen angels and the Devil himself. He will bring the one world religion to the world. The powers that he'll have will deceive all those who are ignorant, and not covered by the blood of Jesus. Those who refuse to take the Mark of the Beast, which is any technology that is implanted in the body for buying and selling, can be saved. Anyone that takes the Mark is doomed. God will allow demons to terrorize as a form of judgement, and to test the faith of man. God wants us to repent and reign with him one thousand years on earth in New Jerusalem.

**2 Thessalonians 2:11** says, "And then shall that Wicked be revealed, whom the Lord shall consume with the spirit of his mouth, and shall destroy with the brightness of his coming:

9. Even him, whose coming is after the working of Satan with all power and signs and lying wonders,

10. And with all deceivableness of unrighteousness in them that perish; because they received not the love of the truth, that they might be saved.

11. And for this cause God shall send them strong delusion, that they should believe a lie:

12. That they all might be damned who believed not the truth, but had pleasure in unrighteousness."

**Mark 13:21** says, "And then if any man shall say to you, Lo, here is Christ; or, lo, he is there; believe him not."

The rainbow that God showed Noah as a promise to never again flood the earth represented Jesus. Read **Revelation 4:3 and 10:1**. This is because the glory of Jesus in Heaven is a cloud and a rainbow. God promised to never destroy the world again by water, but this time it will be with fire. The Father sent his son to save the world. **The rainbow, which is the glory that God clothed him with, is in direct correlation with the coat of many colors Isaac clothed Joseph with.** The perfect correlation of a gift from father to son. Symbolism of glory to the son that saves lives to prevent the inevitable destruction. Joseph saved the people from the inevitable famine. Jesus saves people from the lake of fire.

**Animals symbolize the different types of angels.** Angels have different personalities and purposes the way animals have different personalities and purposes. **Birds represent angels and spirits. Birds can't eat everything on the ground, only what they are allowed to. Spirits can't possess everyone they encounter, only who they're allowed to. Evil Spirits can only inhabit darkness in people. Turn on the light of Christ and you'll be alright.**

**Ephesians 2:2** says, "Wherein in time past ye walked according to the course of this world, according to the prince of the power of the air, the spirit that now worketh in the children of disobedience."

**Job 1:6-12** says, "Now there was a day when the sons of God came to present themselves before the Lord, and Satan came also among them.

7 And the Lord said unto Satan, Whence comest thou? Then Satan answered the Lord, and said, From going to and fro in the earth, and from walking up and down in it. **(The fallen angels had underground cities, caves, and tunnels in many places within the earth, mainly along the equator connecting the northern hemisphere to the southern hemisphere. The fallen angels are eternal and live inside the earth in demensions until they are released as in the book of Revelation. Magma and lava is inside the earth to keep it warm. The fallen angels are reptilian, and reptiles need heat to keep their body temperature regulated. Reptiles are coldblooded so underground with the heat is their habitat. Hell was not designed for man until man provoked God to anger).**

8 And the Lord said unto Satan, Hast thou considered my servant Job, that there is none like him in the earth, a perfect and an upright man, one that feareth God, and escheweth evil?

9 Then Satan answered the Lord, and said, Doth Job fear God for nought?

10 Hast not thou made an hedge about him, and about his house, and about all that he hath on every side? thou hast blessed the work of his hands, and his substance is increased in the land.

11 But put forth thine hand now, and touch all that he hath, and he will curse thee to thy face.

12 And the Lord said unto Satan, Behold, all that he hath is in thy power; only upon himself put not forth thine hand. So Satan went forth from the presence of the Lord."

**The nocturnal animals like bats, owls, rodents, snakes and predators in the animal kingdom represent the demons or fallen angels.** They seek who they may devour in darkness and eat the flesh of other animals. They are dirty scavengers. All reptiles are classified as serpents, and serpents are demons. **Anytime you want to get rid of undesirable animals like roaches, snakes, and other nocturnal animals, just cut the light on. Demons are in darkness, but they leave when you cut the light on with Jesus Christ. Demons are darkness, and darkness can't mix with the light.**

**All Daytime animals have some sort of healthy purpose for man. Either food, symbolism, purpose or pleasure.** They eat from the earth and are meek and humble. Monkeys (primates) resemble man for two reasons. They show man what to eat with a particular intelligence, and that men have a correlation with trees.

**Matthew 7:19** says, "Every tree that bringeth not forth good fruit is hewn down, and cast into the fire."

**John 15:8** says, "Herein is my Father glorified, that ye bear much fruit; so shall ye be my disciples."

**John 15:2** says, "Every branch in me that beareth not fruit he taketh away: and every branch that beareth fruit, he purgeth it, that it may bring forth more fruit."

The largest animals don't eat meat. Bees help pollinate and make honey. Goat's milk is the best. A land flowing with milk and honey has to mean there is much green life, bees, and lamb.

Caterpillars turn into butterflies, but they can't fly without the energy from the sun. When we die, we can't obtain glory without the power of God through his Son. **What's impossible for man is highly possible for God.**

**Revelation 21:23** says, "And the city had no need of the sun, neither of the moon, to shine in it: for the glory of God did lighten it, and the Lamb is the light thereof."

**Revelation 5:13** says, "<u>And every creature which is in heaven, and on the earth, and under the earth, and such as are in the sea, and all that are in them, heard I saying, Blessing, and honour, and glory, and power, be unto him that sitteth upon the throne, and unto the Lamb (Jesus, The Word) for ever and ever.</u>"

# WHY JESUS IS THE NAME THAT HAS POWER

**Revelation 19:12** says, "His eyes were as a flame of fire, and on his head were many crowns; and he had a name written, that no man knew, but he himself."

**Jeremiah 23:26-27** says, "How long shall this be in the heart of the prophets that prophesy lies? yea, they are prophets of the deceit of their own heart; Which think to cause my people to forget my name by their dreams which they tell every man to his neighbour, as their fathers have forgotten my name for Baal."

**Matthew 13:15** says, "For this people's heart is waxed gross, and their ears are dull of hearing, and their eyes they have closed; lest at any time they should see with their eyes and hear with their ears, and should understand with their heart, and should be converted, and I should heal them."

**Acts 17:30** says, "And the times of this ignorance God winked at; but now commandeth all men every where to repent."

**Acts 4:10-12 says,** "Be it known unto you all, and to all the people of Israel, that by the name of Jesus Christ of Nazareth, whom ye crucified, whom God raised from the dead, even by him doth this man stand here before you whole. This is the stone which was set at nought of you builders, which is become the head of the corner. Neither is there salvation in any other: for there is none other name under heaven given among men, whereby we must be saved."

God has many titles and names, even a heavenly name we don't know. Names are only as good as their meaning and truth surrounding the name. Titles define characteristics and attributes. **I have the understanding that God is his word. The truth of his word gives righteousness to the name in his word. God promised to preserve his word, so the name Jesus Christ that is proclaimed in his word is ordained for this dispensation.**

**God demands obedience. Whoever believes in him will have eternal life. Therefore we have to believe that God wouldn't leave us ignorant of his ordained name. The Bible gives the truth of God's word, and if you abide by the Word of God, you can't go wrong. If his word is truth, then the name has to be effective by faith. There is a reason why names were changed in the Bible, and it was according to God's will. What the Devil meant for bad, God meant it for good. As a man believe in his heart so is he. If God's word abides in you, and you believe in your heart that you are calling on the name of the Lord then your faith is accounted for righteousness.**

**1 Peter 1:25** says, "But the word of the Lord endureth for ever. And this is the word which by the gospel is preached unto you."

**Revelation 2:17** says, "He that hath an ear, let him hear what the Spirit saith unto the churches; To him that overcometh will I give to eat of the hidden manna, and will give him a white stone, and in the stone a new name written, which no man knoweth saving he that receiveth it."

**This tells you that belief in God's word gives confirmation to his name because names change, and names are tied to the meaning. Man's accuracy and pronunciation is not as significant as the belief in the name. The name gives identity: however, the identity is the 'Word of God.' I know he had a Hebrew name when he walked on the earth, but God has many names and the one I know has power is 'Jesus.' It's all about belief, and if you believe God preserved his word then you have to believe he will not lead you astray.**

There are various pronunciations and spellings, but names are only as good as what they mean. God created all languages. However, God has preserved his word, and we have to have faith that if his word says Jesus is the only name in which man can be saved, we have to believe it. Why? Because we can't read Hebrew, and how do we know that those who can aren't fabricating a lie to have us calling on Pagan deities according to theology agendas of man? God is love, and love wouldn't leave us without the truth. **I know because I cried out to Jesus, and he heard my cry. I can bear witness that it's power in the name of Jesus. I will help you understand why its power in the name of Jesus.**

**Proverbs 4:7** says, "Wisdom is the principal thing; therefore get wisdom: and with all thy getting get understanding."

**The people in America, who are the descendants of the slaves, are mostly of the tribe of Judah from the 12 tribes of Israel. The Roman army scattered the Israelites into Africa when they raided Jerusalem from 66-70 CE. The Israelites or Jews migrated all over Africa. The Israelites were skilled workers, teachers, and even became Kings and Queens in many countries. Islam was started by Mohammad an Ishmaelite, and he was from**

**Mecca in Saudi Arabia. Islam ruled by sword and forced Israelites to convert or die.** Israelites were in servitude, however some created their own kingdoms. Many Jews converted to Islam in order to stay safe and maintain economic prestige. The result of Islam's conquest became the Ottoman Empire in 1299 and lasted until 1922. Many Israelites migrated to Spain to escape the harsh treatment of the Muslims. In July 1492, Spain expelled its Jews and Muslim populations as part of the Spanish Inquisition. Many Jews fled to Portugal to keep from going back to Africa. The Knights Templar was in Portugal because Portugal was the country in Europe that was lenient on war crimes. The Knights Templar went to Rome to ask the Pope what to do with all the refugees in the land, and they decided to use them as slaves. The Knights Templar and Muslims worked together in capturing Hebrews for the slave trade. With the help of some African moors and Muslims, the Europeans knew exactly where to get all the slaves they could handle. With the bargaining chip of trading guns to particular African leaders, the Europeans were successful in capturing millions of Hebrews from Africa.

The Israelites had Hebrew names when they were in Africa When they came to America every slave had to take on the last name of their slave master, so they could be identified as property to a particular plantation. Today, all of the last names of African Americans go back to the last name of a European, Gentile, slave master. In order to see the evidence of prophecy, you have to understand how Jesus suffered everything his people has to suffer.

The Messiah had a Hebrew name of many variations that people will never be able to agree on. **The messiah took on the gentile name of Jesus the same way African American Hebrews took on a gentile last name that goes back to a gentile slave master. The Messiah had**

**a Hebrew name as his first name, and Jesus was his last name which is a gentile name. However, he ordained the name of Jesus to have the power according to this dispensation.**

**Romans 10:19 says "But I say, Did not Israel know? First Moses saith, I will provoke you to jealousy by them that are no people, and by a foolish nation I will anger you.**

**Romans 11:11 says "I say then, Have they stumbled that they should fall? God forbid: but rather through their fall salvation is come unto the Gentiles, for to provoke them to jealousy.**

**Deuteronomy 28:68 says "And the LORD shall bring thee into Egypt again with ships, by the way whereof I spake unto thee, Thou shalt see it no more again: and there ye shall be sold unto your enemies for bondmen and bondwomen, and no man shall buy you." The bondmen and bondwomen were the Hebrew slaves brought to the Americas on ships by the Europeans, of whom God called, 'their enemies.' Thou shalt see it no more again means, 'You'll never see this form of slavery ever again.' No man shall buy you means, 'No man shall buy your freedom.'**

There has not been a human rights activist that has been able to deliver African Americans from the system of racism and oppression. The system of racism and oppression has only been hidden in plain sight. Only God can deliver us in correlation with how it took God to deliver the Hebrews from ancient Egypt. **The 400 years of slavery in ancient Egypt is a direct correlation with the 400 years of slavery in the spiritual Egypt known as North and South America.** Most of the slaves went to Brazil. The 400 years of slavery mark in the Americas is said to be up around 2019, because the first documented slave was said to be sold in 1619. The timeline doesn't matter, for it is only a sign, however, the will of God does. **We are still in slavery, mentally and physically. They took the 'ation' off of 'Plantation now they call it a 'Plant'. The word went from plantation to plant to trick white and black people to stay on the plantation. What factory or plant do you slave at? Supervisor and the manager is the overseer. You get enough money to get a roof over your head, food, and transportation to get right back on the plantation.**

Now look at the circumstantial correlation between Jesus and Israel. **The Hebrew slaves of the Atlantic slave trade, were betrayed by their own people, captured, lynched, and hung on a tree. Jesus was a Hebrew that was betrayed by his own people, captured, lynched, and hung on a tree. Judas didn't fully understand what he was doing when he betrayed Jesus, for he just wanted money. The Africans and Muslims didn't fully understand what they were doing in betraying the Hebrew slaves, they just wanted guns. Judas didn't really understand what he was doing when he betrayed Jesus, he just wanted thirty pieces of silver. The same thing that happened to Jesus happened to his people. This fulfills prophecy.**

**Psalm 111:6** says, "He hath shewed his people the power of his works, that he may give them the heritage of the heathen."

**Jeremiah 17:4** says, "Even thyself, (meaning God himself) shalt discontinue from thine heritage and I will cause thee to serve thine enemies in the land which thou knowest not."

**Jeremiah 12:7** says, "I have forsaken mine house, I have left mine heritage; I have given the dearly beloved of my soul into the hand of her enemies."

**Gelatians 3:13** says "Christ hath redeemed us from the curse of the law, being made a curse for us: for it is written, cursed is every one that hangeth on a tree."

The same thing that happened to the Messiah happened to his people. Betrayed, captured, lynched, and hung on a tree. Then went from a Hebrew name to a Gentile name. From his Hebrew name to Jesus. Consider the movie Roots. From Kunta Kenta to Toby. Every Negro in America has a last name that goes back to a gentile slave master. Even God himself took on a Gentile name which fulfills the prophecy of Jeremiah 17:4 & Jeremiah 12:7. **That's why its power in the name of Jesus because the 'J' sound in Hebrew wasn't incorporated until years after the crucifixion.**

The people that translated the Bible was not allowed by God to change the content of the scriptures for deception. All they wanted to do was change some names to fit a European heritage. **God allowed names to be changed in the New Testament to give the "Illusion" that Hebrews were white people, in correlation with the pictures Leonardo painted, to deceive people, allowing people to believe Jesus was white. The content of the King James Version is how God wanted it to be. The only alters were name translations to fit the European, gentile image.** God gave the glory of the gospel to the gentiles. Look at the names in the Old Testament then look at the New Testament. That was allowed by God, so that his heritage, the Hebrews, would appear to be European. This had to occur in order for the power to shift to the Gentiles. Without the Gentiles having the perception of Godlike favor, the curses ordained for the Israelites wouldn't have had the support of Europeans.

**Isaiah 42:16** says, "And I will bring the blind by a way that they knew not; I will lead them in paths that they have not known: I will make darkness light before them, and crooked things straight." These things will I do unto them, and not forsake them."

**Romans 11:25** says, "For I would not, brethren, that ye should be ignorant of this mystery, lest ye should be wise in your own conceits; that blindness in part is happened to Israel, until the fulness of the Gentiles be come in."

**The key is that he has not forsaken his heritage. God has chosen the foolish things to confound the wise, and the weak things to confound the things that are mighty. God let us be blind in order to teach us a lesson for us to be humble, and for us to stop taking the power of God for granted and fear him to keep his commandments.**

**Ephesians 3:1-9 says, "**For this cause I Paul, the prisoner of Jesus Christ for you Gentiles,

2. If ye have heard of the dispensation of the grace of God which is given me to you-ward:

3. How that by revelation he made known unto me the mystery; (as I wrote afore in few words,

4. Whereby, when ye read, ye may understand my knowledge in the mystery of Christ

5. Which in other ages was not made known unto the sons of men, as it is now revealed unto his holy apostles and prophets by the Spirit;

6. That the Gentiles should be fellow heirs, and of the same body, and partakers of his promise in Christ by the gospel:

7. Whereof I was made a minister, according to the gift of the grace of God given unto me by the effectual working of his power.

8. Unto me, who am less than the least of all saints, is this grace given, that I should preach among the Gentiles the unsearchable riches of Christ;

9. And to make all men see what is the fellowship of the mystery, which from the beginning of the world hath been hid in God, who created all things by Jesus Christ."

**Names are only good for what they mean. No matter what your name is, if you believe that it means something, then that's what it means.** As a man believeth in his heart, so is he. God changed Abram's name to Abraham and Saul's name to Paul. Abraham started the law of circumcision. Moses had the Ten Commandments and law which was committed to Israel. Paul spread the gospel of grace that was given to the gentiles. The Gentiles have spread the Gospel of Jesus all over the world. God has many earthly names, but a heavenly name that no one knows. Jesus is definitely the name of the Messiah according to this dispensation. I believe the gentile name Jesus holds the power because God left his heritage, like he said, to become the God of the Gentiles and the Jews, salvation for all who believe, showing no respect for persons. The first shall be last, and the last shall be first.

**Jeremiah 12:8** says, "Mine heritage is unto me as a lion in the forest; it crieth out against me: therefore have I hated it." God gave his heritage to the Gentiles, and it was ordained through the curse that African Americans would be ignorant concerning their heritage. According to **Isaiah 42:16,** God said that he would lead us in paths that we have not known. He said he would make darkness light before us, and crooked things straight. **Ecclesiastes 7:13** says, "Consider the work of God: for who can make that straight, which he hath made crooked?" Read **Romans 1**. It says that even when they knew God they still went after the lust of the flesh serving other gods. God said, "Therefore I have hated my heritage."

Moreover, God is always faithful to forgive, and he is waiting for us to get the big picture and repent. Not only the sins we've committed, but we have to break the generational curses we inherited from our for-fathers, by sincerely being born again spiritually through Jesus Christ. **The curse is simply the law "reap what you sow" in effect. The curse is a humbling mechanism that makes us realize that we all reap what we sow.** Our actions always matter, for they can open a door for a curse. Jesus is the way, truth, and life. The way to the truth that sets you free, and freedom is in the mind, which leads to eternal life. Way, truth, and life.

**Luke 21:24** says, "And they shall fall by the edge of the sword, and shall be led away captive into all nations: and Jerusalem shall be trodden down of the Gentiles, until the times of the Gentiles be fulfilled."

***The times of the Gentiles is almost fulfilled***

Jerusalem has been trodden down of the Gentiles, because the people in Israel today are Europeans and

Russians (Edomites). They are actually Khazarians from Khazaria, the land between Europe and Russia. The Khazarians were traders and soldiers that played a key commercial role as a crossroad between China, the Middle East and Kievan Rus' (Belarus, Ukraine, and Russia all claim Kievan Rus' as their cultural ancestors). Just like the Roman Emperor, the Khazarians adopted the heritage of the Hebrews to give them justification for their endeavors. The main goal is to cut Israel off from becoming a nation.

Psalm 2

1. Why do the heathen rage, and the people imagine a vain thing?

2. The kings of the earth set themselves, and the rulers take counsel together, against the LORD, and against his anointed, saying,

3. Let us break their bands asunder, and cast away their cords from us.

4. He that sitteth in the heavens shall laugh: the Lord shall have them in derision.

5. Then shall he speak unto them in his wrath, and vex them in his sore displeasure.

**True Israel are who we call niggers, negroes, black, and African Americans. Not just in America, but scattered all over the world mixed with all nationalities. Captivity, servitude, slavery, and migration has always been the vehicle in which Abraham's seed has been scattered among all nations. Jew is just a gentile word for 'Judah', but in the Hebrew tongue 'Yahudah'.**

**Luke 13:30** says, "And, behold, there are last which shall be first, and there are first which shall be last."

Jesus was first, then made himself last, then became first again. Black people were first, and white people were last. God made white people first, and black people last, so that all those in faith may become first in spirit by humility and being obedient to God. **Israel is called to be a light unto the gentiles. For this understanding is humbling knowing all has been allowed by the hand of God in order for all man to fear God.**

**1 Peter 5:5** says, "Likewise, ye younger, submit yourselves unto the elder. Yea, all of you be subject one to another, and be clothed with humility: for God resisteth the proud, and giveth grace to the humble."

**Proverbs 1:7** says, "The fear of the Lord is the beginning of knowledge: but fools despise wisdom and instruction."

**2 Chronicles 7:14** says, "If my people, which are called by my name, shall humble themselves, and pray, and seek my face, and turn from their wicked ways; then will I hear from heaven, and will forgive their sin, and will heal their land." **(Notice that the first thing God said we have to do is humble ourselves. God doesn't have to punish us himself. All he has to do is take some of his protection off of us, and demons will have the opportunity to attack on whatever level God allows them to. The book of Job holds the example.)**

The Messiah went by a Hebrew name that is tied to his Hebrew heritage. Now he answers to Jesus that has a gentile heritage. The same way African American Hebrews answer to their gentile last names although it's not tied to the

Hebrew heritage. Some have African first names, but our last names are always gentile names going back to the slave master. **God's first name was Hebrew, and Jesus is his last name, in direct correlation to African American Hebrews that pick an African name for their first name, but remain with the gentile last name.**

**I have an African (Swahili) first and middle name that means "He Who Walks With God", my middle name means "Brilliant", but my last name goes back to a slaver master.** If you're wondering who I really am and what my credentials are for this understanding I am imparting onto you, just understand **Proverbs 22:1** that says, "A good name is rather to be chosen than great riches, and loving favour rather than silver and gold." Don't worry about my name because it's only as good as what it means. As a man believeth in his heart so is he.

Cassius Clay didn't like the idea of having a gentile name, that's why he changed it to Mahammad Ali. Cassius Clay is Mahammad Ali, and Mahammad Ali is Cassius Clay, BUT, he answers only to Mahammad Ali. **Jesus went through the same things his people went through, as a sign, so Israel can know who they are solidifying that God is in control and his word is true, also realizing how much God loves and wants the children of Abraham to come back to him.**

Who God loves he corrects. The black man wouldn't have reaped punishment if their for-fathers didn't sow it. History is a sign that fulfills the prophecy, "The first shall be last and the last shall be first." **If you desire to be first, you have to be last. Jesus made himself last so that he would be first again. Black people were first, God made them last, so they can become first again. Not first in flesh, but**

**first in spirit. Oppression makes a man cry out to God. Pride makes a man rely on his own devices.**

**Acts 13:47** says, "For so hath the Lord commanded us, saying, I have set thee to be a light of the Gentiles, that thou shouldest be for salvation unto the ends of the earth."

**Matthew 5:3** says, "Blessed are the poor in spirit: for theirs is the kingdom of heaven."

Israel have been on the bottom for a long time now. The Kingdom of Heaven is at hand in Jesus Christ name.

# THE BIBLE IS THE TRUE WORD OF PROPHECY

### Why Black Women Wear Wigs and Weave and get Fibroids

**Isaiah 3:16** says, "Moreover the Lord saith, Because the daughters of Zion are haughty, and walk with stretched forth necks and wanton eyes, walking and mincing as they go, and making a tinkling with their feet: Therefore the Lord will smite with a **scab the crown of the head** of the daughters of Zion, and thc **Lord will discover their secret parts.**"

(If it wasn't for the pressure of trying to fit into mainstream society with white people, black women wouldn't **perm their hair, which kills hair**. Perms can cause **baldness**, damage hair follicles, and also cause **fibroids**. **Check this out! Fibroids end up in the Uterus. The uterus is their secret parts.)**

### The Wheel was Invented Before the Flood, but I Believe There is Even a Prophecy About Cars

**Isaiah 3:18** says, "In that day the Lord will take away the bravery of their tinkling ornaments about their feet, and their cauls, and their **round tires like the moon**."

**(Could round tires like the moon be 24 inch rims?** You tell me.)

**Isaiah 3:19** says, "The chains, and the bracelets, and the **mufflers**."

(Loud pipes big rims shawdy that our life, which was quoted in a rap song in which promotes jewelry and the lavish things of the world). The Lord will take away the chains, bracelets, and the mufflers. Bling bling gone bad. **I don't know anything that has a muffler besides a car. Electric cars dont have mufflers. That prophecy has been knocking on our door for a while now.** Store your treasure in heaven, let God manage it, goods on earth tarnish and vanishes.

## This is Why Judah Hang on the Street Corner

**Isaiah 51:20** says, "Thy sons have fainted, **they lie at the head of all the streets**, as a wild bull in a net: they are full of the fury of the Lord, the rebuke of thy God."

Fainted means, "You've lost your mind." Wild bull in a net means, "You feel trapped." Like Master P said, "Trapped in the dope game." **Israel is deceived to believe that there is no positive avenue to exert energy so it goes into an endless cycle of sin and vanity.** Many people blame God for their poverty and miss-happenings, but never considering its God's way of ridding the pride and having us depend totally on him instead of Satan's devices. That's why the Hebrew slaves were in the wilderness, and that's where we are now. **Matthew 18:3** says "Except ye be converted, and become as little children, ye shall not enter into the kingdom of heaven." Children are totally dependent on their parents, and God wants us totally dependent on him. The older generation died off and the children were able to take the promised land. **Matthew 5:3** says "Blessed are the poor in spirit: for theirs is the kingdom of heaven." The rich get their reward on Earth, but the poor in the Holy Spirit get eternal paradise. **Matthew 19:24**, Mark **10:25**, and **Luke 18:25** says, "It is easier for a camel to go through the eye of a needle, than for a rich man to enter into the kingdom of God." **The eye of a needle, by the way, was a thin hole in a city wall where only one man could come through. Therefore, if an army invaded, only one soldier could come into the city at a time making the front easy to defend. Matthew 6:20** says, "But lay up for yourselves treasures in heaven, where neither moth nor rust doth corrupt, and where thieves do not break through nor steal."

Poverty is God's way of keeping us dependent on him. God wants us to be humble, and prosperity makes people comfortable with being disobedient to God. They feel like they don't need God. They become their own god. **What profits a man to gain the world and loose his soul?** Gods ways are not our ways, neither his thoughts our thoughts. God has blessed the descendants of Abraham by not allowing them to obtain too much materialistic stuff, making it easier for them to obtain eternal treasure. Read **Job 33:16-18 says "Then he openeth the ears of men, and sealeth their instruction, That he may withdraw man from his purpose, and hide pride from man.** He keepeth back his soul from the pit, and his life from perishing by the sword.

David's son King Solomon was the richest man that ever lived and although God blessed him in abundance with wisdom and riches, women and prosperity was the catalyst that made him comfortable with disobeying God. Without the prosperity, he wouldn't have had 300 wives and 700 concubines. **Solomon indulged in everything there is to do in life and came to the conclusion that all is vanity and vexation of spirit.**

**Psalm 12:8 says, "The wicked walk on every side, when the vilest men are exalted."** When sin is rewarded with riches, everybody that sees becomes influenced and desensitized. Our society puts emphasis on the love of money, and that appeals to our pride, causing us to do unethical things for money, which leads to our destruction. **God wants us to use the gifts that he gave us to prosper and serve well. Good service will always sustain life.** Jesus came to be a servant. You have to be humble and comfortable being last before being elevated to first. **Have to be a follower before a leader, and a servant before a master, so that you don't take your power for granted and disrespect servitude. Job 8:7 says "Though thy beginning was small, yet thy latter end should greatly increase."**

**Revelation 2:9** says "I know thy works, and tribulation, and poverty, (but thou art rich) and I know the blasphemy of them which say they are Jews, and are not, but are the synagogue of Satan." **God is saying that the real Jews are actually in poverty and is going through tribulation, and those in power that claim to be Jews are the synagogue of Satan.** But thou art rich means that the real Jews are rich within. **They have all the spiritual, and physical gifts more so than any people in the world.** For example: Michael Jordan, Mahammad Ali, Serena Williams, and Dr. King etc…Listen to all Dr. King's speeches, and read the letter from the Birmingham jail. Dr. King was a prophet. Use your gifts to glorify God and sustain life.

**1 Peter 3:17** says, "For it is better, if the will of God be so, that ye suffer for well doing, than for evil doing."

**Romans 3:1-2 says, "What advantage then hath the Jew, or what profit is there of circumcision? Much**

**every way: chiefly, because that unto the Jews were committed the oracles of God."**

# HOW WE ARE STILL ENSLAVED

## (Plant = Plantation)

## (Supervisor and Manager is the Overseer)

**They call industrial factories plants because plant is short for plantation.** The industrial world is just a huge plantation. Social Security was the number Americans received that made us property and collateral. The American government put the people up as collateral for the debt owed to the Private European bankers who tricked us into accepting the dollar as our money currency, and loaning us money they knew we couldn't pay back in order to create a debt based society. This way independent gangster bankers Americans don't even know, through the power of debt, can own the country's sovereignty.

The birth certificate of every American is worth a ton of money on the New York Stock Exchange. One of the most famous elitest banker said, "Let me control the money of a country and I care not who makes its laws." That's because whomever owns the money can buy off the politicians. The world is overwhelmingly evil because the love of money is the root of all evil. We got out of the Great Depression by the American people becoming property of the Private Banking cabal, through Social Security. They see us as human resources. We are legally classified as property of the corporation of America, and as collateral for debt.

**Under the law, corporations have to have a president and a secretary of treasure. The U.S. is a**

**corporation, not a country. Countries have Kings. Corporations have presidents and secretaries of treasure. Our worth is measured by the taxes we can contribute to pay for debt we didn't create in the first place.**

Our society is not under the law of the land. We are under Maritime Admiralty Law, which is the law of water. The prefix 'Mer' stands for sea creatures. That's where the word 'mermaid' comes from. We are under the law of water, which is tied to Dagon or the water kingdom spirits. The ancient pagan god Dagon, is one of the gods of the Vatican. Dagon was a half fish - half man. That's why they wear the fish-head-hats in the Vatican. The fish-head-hat represents the god Dagon. Mermaids symbolize Dagon.

**Judges 16:23** says, "Then the lords of the Philistines gathered them together for to offer a great sacrifice unto Dagon their god, and to rejoice: for they said, Our god hath delivered Samson our enemy into our hand."

**1 Samuel 5:4** says, "And when they arose early on the morrow morning, behold, Dagon was fallen upon his face to the ground before the ark of the Lord; and the head of Dagon and both the palms of his hands were cut off upon the threshold; only the stump of Dagon was left to him."

The ships that were sailed across the sea by merchants used a flag to represent the law of the country that each particular ship was sovereign to. This was to make sure people knew the law they were under upon boarding a particular ship. That's why Maritime Admiralty Law is the law of water.

We call money currency because a river has a current. The current of the river is directed by the river bank. That's why we put our currency in a bank. When products come off of a ship, they unload it at the doc. Every product has a certificate of manifest. The certificate of manifest tells the merchant everything about the product including its worth. When we are born, our mother's water breaks. We are born out of the water into the hands of the doc or doctor. Every child born in our society receives a birth certificate (certificate of manifest). Our birth certificate tells Wall Street everything about us including our worth.

We only have safety precautions and insurance, because our body is worth money on Wall Street. Everything in our society is based on money. Money is water. Water has a current. Currents never stop flowing. That's why we have cash flow. Every aspect of our life cost money keeping us in a constant state of survival. The constant state of survival blinds us from who we are and why we are here. That confirms the fact that we are still slaves. When people are dependant on

God is about to do something about it. He's wants people to realize who they are, repent, pray, and seek his face. Quit worrying about the evil going on and focus on the good that's coming. Let not your hearts be troubled. **New Jerusalem is the new promise land.** Read about New Jerusalem in **Revelations 21**. It's iced out. The whole city is on bling for real. **Man started in Africa where all the gold, silver, diamonds and every natural resource is, and the men who are saved by God thru grace will end up where all the Gold and precious stones are for eternity.**

# THE REASON WHY ISRAEL WAS PUNISHED WITH SLAVERY

**Deuteronomy 28:1-2/15-16** says, "And it shall come to pass, if thou shalt hearken diligently unto the voice of the LORD thy God, to observe and to do all his commandments which I command thee this day, that the LORD thy God will set thee on high above all nations of the earth:

2. And all these blessings shall come on thee, and overtake thee, if thou shalt hearken unto the voice of the LORD thy God.

15. But it shall come to pass, if thou wilt not hearken unto the voice of the LORD thy God, to observe to do all his commandments and his statutes which I command thee this day; that all these curses shall come upon thee, and overtake thee:

16. Cursed shalt thou be in the city, and cursed shalt thou be in the field."

**Deuteronomy 28:68 says, "And the Lord shall bring thee into Egypt again with ships, by the way whereof I spake unto thee, Thou shalt see it no more again: and there ye shall be sold unto your enemies for bondmen and bondwomen, and no man shall buy you." (28:68) (2+6 = 8) (8 x 8 x 8 = 512) (5 + 1 + 2 = 8)**

**8 is the number of eternity. It makes a continuous curve from top to bottom, from bottom to top. What happened then has nothing on what will happen later if we don't repent.**

**Deuteronomy 9:6** says, "Understand therefore, that the Lord thy God giveth thee not this good land to possess it for thy righteousness; for thou art a stiffnecked people."

**God allowed his people to go into slavery as a way of correction and punishment for disobeying his laws statues and commandments. They were worshiping other pagan gods, which we're falling angels, hybrids, and channeling evil spirits just like our black celeberties are today. We know more about these pagan holidays than the holidays God gave us in the Bible. Every holiday in our culture today is a demonic initiation.**

**When the hybrids were on earth, people worshiped them and their fathers as gods.** Greek mythology white washed the Egyptian gods, and the Egyptians got their gods from Babylon during the time of Nimrod. In todays culture, we have the same gods disguised as super heros like Spider Man and the Black Panther.

In the culture of the pagan Africans, they would invoke a demonic spirit into almost any object or artifact wood or stone as worship. In voodoo they channel spirits into dolls or whatever. **Most Catholic artifacts dedicated to white-washed saints have spirits channeled into them and sold in stores for people to take home.**

**Wisdom of Solomon 13:10** says, "**But miserable are they, and in dead things is their hope, who call them gods, which are the works of men's hands, gold and silver, to shew art in, and resemblances of beasts, or a stone good for nothing, the work of an ancient hand.**

**I have an African friend that told me never to bring African art into your house because you never know if a spirit is tied to it.** He had a friend that had African art work on his wall. Their marriage began to go downhill. They sought spiritual counselling and was instructed to pray together in the living room to rid any spiritual influence that was coming against their marriage. One day while they was praying, the spirit attached to the artwork communicated with them to say, "I don't want to be here." They asked the spirit what his name was and it told them. They got rid of that particular art work and their marriage has been better ever since. No way would I make that up. **There are still some black people that teach channeling the spirit of ancestors, but all that is doing is channeling demons.**

**Anyway, the Hebrews went into slavery because of them practicing sorcery and witchcraft like voodoo, enchantments, soothsaying, tarot cards, and along with the abundance of sin, pride, lust, and pure disobedience.** God is a jealous God because he wants us to worship him instead of demons and idols. It's like a father jealous of another man because his daughter calls another man 'Daddy.'

**Deuteronomy 29:17** says, "And ye have seen their abominations, and their idols, wood and stone, silver and gold, which were among them."

**Isaiah 37:19** says "And have cast their gods into the fire: for they were no gods, but the work of men's hands, wood and stone: therefore they have destroyed them."

**Daniel 5:32** says "But hast lifted up thyself against the Lord of heaven; and they have brought the vessels of his house before thee, and thou, and thy lords, thy wives, and thy concubines, have drunk wine in them; and thou hast praised the gods of silver, and gold, of brass, iron, wood, and stone, which see not, nor hear, nor know: and the God in whose hand thy breath is, and whose are all thy ways, hast thou not glorified."

**Job 27:13** says, "This is the portion of a wicked man with God, and the heritage of oppressors, which they shall receive of the Almighty."

**Psalm 111:6** says, "He hath shewed his people the power of his works, that he may give them the heritage of the heathen."

**Jeremiah 12:7** says, "I have forsaken mine house, I have left mine heritage; I have given the dearly beloved of my soul into the hand of her enemies."

**Jeremiah 12:8** says, "Mine heritage is unto me as a lion in the forest; it crieth out against me: therefore have I hated it."

**Jeremiah 17:4** says, "And thou, even thyself, shalt discontinue from thine heritage that I gave thee; and I will cause thee to serve thine enemies in the land which thou knowest not: for ye have kindled a fire in mine anger, which shall burn forever."

**Joel 2:17** says, "Let the priests, the ministers of the Lord, weep between the porch and the altar, and let them say, Spare thy people, O Lord, and give not thine heritage to reproach, that the heathen should rule over them: wherefore should they say among the people, Where is their God?"

**Micah 7:18** says, "Who is a God like unto thee, that pardoneth iniquity, and passeth by the transgression of the remnant of his heritage? He retaineth not his anger for ever, because he delighteth in mercy."

# WHERE WE ARE AT TODAY

**The Lord delivered the Israelites out of slavery in ancient Egypt. The almighty God wanted the Israelites to realize that his power was supreme power over the demonic sorcery and witchcraft power of the Egyptians. The Lord then led them into the wilderness for their faith to be tested**. God wanted to groom them, and purge them from their slave mentality. God wanted the Israelites to trust in him with all their heart, and know that God was on their side. When it was time to go into the promised land, those hybrid giants of the fallen angels were in the land. God said that it was the land he promised them and they could take the land, but the Israelites forbid them to take the land out of fear. The fear, slave mentality, and mistrust, left God with no choice but to wait until they die off, and let their children, who had never been slaves, take the land.

**The reason God commanded Joshua to kill everyone when they went to war, was because the giant hybrids of the fallen angels were on the land. Today we still have giants that we have to face. New Jerusalem that will come down from heaven, is our New Promise land.** In America, all the people that endured the brutality had already died off. Now, we have a new generation that knows not the slavery of old, but the slavery of mind control and demonic influence. However, this time we have to fight a spiritual war. **We don't wrestle against flesh and blood, but powers, principalities, rulers of the darkness of this age, and spiritual wickedness in high places. We need the Holy Spirit to fight evil spirits.**

**Jude 1:5** says "I will therefore put you in remembrance, though ye once knew this, how that the Lord, having saved the people out of the land of Egypt, afterward destroyed them that believed not."

**Romans 1** reads, "Because that, when they knew God, they glorified him not as God, neither were thankful; but became vain in their imaginations, and their foolish heart was darkened. Professing themselves to be wise, they became fools, and changed the glory of the incorruptible God into an image made like to corruptible man, and to birds, and four-footed beasts, and creeping things. **Wherefore God also gave them up to uncleanness through the lusts of their own hearts, to dishonor their own bodies between themselves:** Who changed the truth of God into a lie, and worshipped and served the creature more than the Creator, who is blessed forever. Amen." For this cause God gave them up unto vile **(wretchedly bad)** affections: **for even their women did change the natural use into that which is against nature: And likewise also the men, leaving the natural use of the woman, burned in their lust one toward another; men with men working that which is unseemly**, and receiving in themselves that recompense of their error which was meet."

(Recompense means: to pay or give compensation for; make restitution.) (Meet means encountered.) Meaning they receive in themselves the payment of their error that they encountered. And even as they did not like to retain God in their knowledge, God gave them over to a reprobate mind, to do those things which are not convenient." **Definition of 'Not convenient': (Not)** suitable or **(Not)** agreeable to the needs or purpose or **(Not)** ease in use; **(Not)** favorable, **(Not)** easy, or **(Not)** comfortable for use, And **(Not)** well-suited with respect.

Men that take the part of their body that gives life, and you put in in the part of the body that symbolizes death or waist, where parasites, toxins, and bacteria live. **That cannot be agreeable to the needs or purpose, and absolutely cannot be comfortable for use.**

# EXPLAINATION OF WHAT A CURSE REALIY IS

**A curse is simply subject to God's law, "You reap what you sow."** The curse is the mechanism that makes creation less and less like heaven. The more disobedient a child is, the more punishment increases to yield the child to obedience. The sins of parents fall on their children, as we know as a generational curse.

**A curse is simply sin that remains in the genetics (book of life) of people who are not born again and purged from all iniquity.** Being born again of the Holy Spirit strips the curse from our genetics. However, we are all born in sin. Some people have protection from God in certain areas and only inherit certain curses. **A curse can also occur from the lack of protection from God.** We can have protection in some areas, but no protection in other areas depending on the doors we open. God made Adam and Eve perfect. Curses create the lack of perfection. Heaven is perfection. On Earth as it is in Heaven. Sin made Earth less and less like Heaven.

Most every mental illness is demon possession that results from the lack of God's protection. All of our forfather's sins remain in our genetics for up to four generations. God gives everyone gifts; spiritual and physical gifts. Our gifts are to be used to help us deal with the curses we inherit. **Therefore, we all are products of the gift and the curse.**

**Being forced into slavery is the lack of protection from God.** The torment God allowed the Devil to bring on Job was a result of the lack of protection from God. A child born into slavery inherits a curse from the actions of for-fathers. **Slavery is not good just because a child is born into it. Homosexuality is not good, just because a child is born into it.** If a person is born a homosexual, that person inherited a generational curse. Someone in his/her genetic line was sexually perverted and the sin remains in the genetics. Most people get molested as children and get possessed by that perverted demon. Some people simply open the door to be possessed by that perverted demon, and find themselves given over to a reprobate mind to do those things that are not convenient. Then they end up passing on that sin to their children if they happen to have any. This is why most children suffer from the same strongholds as their parents, whether it's disease, greed, pride, disobedience, addiction, or homosexuality. This is why everyone has a weakness somewhere. **The curse is a humbling mechanism that is designed to help us understand the results of sin, and why pride is so dangerous. Jesus, who knew no sin, became sin for us, and died for us, so that through him we can break the curse and have power over the demons we encounter every day.**

## DEUTERONOMY 28 – BLESSINGS OR CURSES

*****(Matthew 18:7** says, **"<u>Woe unto the world because of offences! For it must needs be that offences come; but woe to that man by whom the offence cometh!</u>")*****

**Deuteronomy 28:30** says, "<u>Thou shalt betroth a wife, and another man shall lie with her: thou shalt build a</u>

house, and thou shalt not dwell therein: thou shalt plant a vineyard, and shalt not gather the grapes thereof."

**(Whether the slaves got married or not, the slave master used the women for sex whenever and however they wanted. The slaves didn't benefit from any of their labor. They was worked until death.)**

**V-32.** "Thy sons and thy daughters shall be given unto another people, and thine eyes shall look, and fail with longing for them all the day long; and there shall be no might in thine hand."

**(When the slaves had children, the slave masters would sell them off to whomever if they deemed it profitable enough. They bread the slaves like cattle because they were worth money, and it was nothing the Hebrews parents could do about it.)**

**V-37**. "And thou shalt become an **astonishment**, a **proverb**, and a **byword**, among all nations whither the LORD shall lead thee."

**(That byword is nigger and negro. Byword definition is: a word or phrase associated with some person or thing; a characteristic expression, typical greeting, or the like. A word or phrase used proverbially; common saying; proverb. An object of general reproach, derision, scorn, etc...)**

**V-41.** "Thou shalt beget sons and daughters, but thou shalt not enjoy them; for they shall go into captivity."

**V-43.** "The stranger that is within thee shall get up above thee very high; and thou shalt come down very low."

**V-44.** "He shall lend to thee, and thou shalt not lend to him: he shall be the head, and thou shalt be the tail."

**(Black people don't have any institution of business for wealth to sustain its own people.** They are economically at the mercy of everyone else. Indians and Arabs have all the stores and hotels in the inner cities. Chinese, Mexican restaurants etc… Very seldom see a soul food restaurant. Hebrews don't have banks or hospitals. Professional ball players have white agents that manage their money making sure it isn't used for the betterment of the people. Sports is nothing but the Roman Coliseum. **Every black man that gets rich, the power elite program them into the ongoing cycle of greed and direct their ambitions into any and everything else besides the betterment of black people.** Koreans even sell black women wigs and weaves.)

**V-46.** "And they shall be upon thee for a sign and for a wonder, and upon thy seed forever."

**(These curses shall be for a sign. No people in the world can identify with all of these curses but African Americans.)**

**V-48.** "Therefore shalt thou serve thine enemies which the LORD shall send against thee, in hunger, and in thirst, and in nakedness, and in want of all things: and he shall put a yoke of iron upon thy neck, until he have destroyed thee."

**(The slaves were taken captive naked with iron chains bound by their neck, hands, and feet)**

**V-49.** "The LORD shall bring a nation against thee from far, from the end of the earth, as swift as the eagle flieth; a nation whose tongue thou shalt not understand;"

**V-50.** "A nation of fierce countenance, which shall not regard the person of the old, nor shew favour to the young."

**V-60.** "Moreover he will bring upon thee all the diseases of Egypt, which thou wast afraid of; and they shall cleave unto thee."

**V-61.** "Also every sickness, and every plague, which is not written in the book of this law, them will the LORD bring upon thee, until thou be destroyed."

**European history consists of one disease after another.** One example is the bubonic plague in Europe that killed up to 200 million from 1347 to 1351. Small pox killed the Native Americans in mass numbers. Today diseases are manufactured in a lab and distributed through vaccinations. Aids, Ebola, Polio, West Nile, SARS, Lyme Disease, Spanish and Swine flu (H1N1), Syphilis, and everything else that we thought was natural but was created. **God didn't create a hole in your body for a needle to go.** Leave vaccinations alone. Eat herbs. The herbs are natural medicine. From thousands of herbs, there are very few herbs or fruit native to Europe and Russia. God subjected white people to land that didn't have much medicine.)

**V-68.** "And the LORD shall bring thee into Egypt again with ships, by the way whereof I spake unto thee, Thou shalt see it no more again: and there ye shall be sold unto your enemies for bondmen and bondwomen, and no man shall buy you."

**(This is the slavery we are still in today, because social security is what made the people collateral for America to the Big Bankers we are in debt to.** The bankers in Europe tricked America into getting in debt we couldn't pay off, which caused the Great Depression in the 1930's. The Social Security Number made us the property of the Private Bankers the same way slaves were property of the Planter Elite. Their mission is to depopulate and enslave the human race. Use racial tension to distract everybody along with war, entertainment, (sports, music, movies, shows, and video games), crime, politics and class, while the Power elite steal and control all the resources we need for human survival. We are still in slavery with the illusion of freedom. "No man shall buy you" means 'no man shall save you'; meaning only God will deliver us. We don't have the physical tools to resist. They have all the bombs, and the people are unorganized. There is a way that seems right to a man, but the end is destruction. Freedom comes by the Spirit of God. Free from sin, demons, strongholds, but with the ability to love. **God is love, and we can't truly love without God. Most people mistake love with affection, but love is actually praying for people, charity, and leading people to Jesus.)**

# FROM THE APOSTLES TO THE KNIGHTS TEMPLAR

Paul the apostle was a Hebrew. He spoke several languages and was highly intelligent. At first he was working for the government, which at that time was the Roman Empire. The environment at the time was pagan, religious, and political. **The Hebrews or the Jews were used to the traditional Law of Abraham and Moses. Jesus came and died for our sins so that we didn't need to go to a priest and make sacrifices for sin anymore.** Those that saw Jesus perform miracles were the ones who believed that Jesus was the true son of God. The gospel of Jesus was considered an abomination to those Pharisees that were used to the traditional belief system. They had religious institutions that they were getting rich off of, and the gospel of Jesus would make their institutions obsolete. By making the gospel popular would endanger the lives of those people who were in jurisdiction of the Roman Empire and or the Pharisees and Sadducees. The King was considered a god and the earth was his Kingdom (same tradition the Pope continues). They also had a pagan belief system that had a god for everything. Their gods were fallen angels (Nephilim), and the hybrids. Jesus demonstrated to people that he was God, and that was blasphemy to the King of the Roman Empire, however it was the Pharisees that saw Jesus as the greatest threat. The Pharisees are those that pressured the King to have Jesus crucified. The Roman soldiers and the governmental institution would persecute anyone who came against Roman law. **Paul was persecuting the Jews for the testimony of Jesus, because he believed the gospel of Jesus was blasphemy against the traditional Law of Moses.** After Jesus had died on the cross for the sins of man, he revealed himself to Paul on the road to Damascus. Yahushua caused Paul to be blind for a while, so when he obtained his sight he would be able to see spiritually. Jesus poured the essence of his love into Paul and chose him to take his gospel to the gentiles in Europe. **God knew that his people were spoiled, but the Gentiles and Europeans were hungry for the truth.** Paul used his intelligence and wisdom to effectively get the word of God to the gentiles around Europe. He suffered much persecution, but he knew the God of all creation and understood that our present sufferings do not compare to the glory that will be revealed in us through Christ Jesus.

**Psalm 111:6** says, "He hath shewed his people the power of his works, that he may give them the heritage of the heathen."

**When the Europeans caught wind of the gospel of Jesus, they loved it. The people were willing to die for the gospel of Jesus. The Roman Emperor Constantinople realized that the gospel was the most powerful thing he'd ever seen. He figured that if he accepted the gospel into his society, he could be the ruler over the gospel and tell people only what he wanted them to know.** He called the gospel Christianity, and made himself the ruler over Christianity. The King realized that in order to rule the world, he had to control the belief system or the religion of people. **All the religions and belief systems originated from fallen angel and were given to black rulers. The Europeans took those spiritual systems and white washed them. The Bible is not a religion, the bible is the truth. However, God allowed Europeans to white wash the Bible with imagery and gentile names. He realized that all the natural resources and riches are on land first inhabited by melanated people. In order to rule the world, the spiritual belief system of melanated people**

**have to be controlled.** The Roman Army didn't want to invade Jerusalem at first because the people in the region were black like the Messiah. It wasn't until the Vatican white washed the Bible to desensitize Europeans on killing black Jews. The Roman army went on crusades to raid and confiscate as much wealth and knowledge as they possibly could from southern lands inhabited by black people. Soloman's temple was raided along with the library of Alexandria in Egypt. Islam or the Ottomans gained control of the land later. Then the Knights Templar began their crusades to take the land, but the muslims put up an intolerable fight. After a while Rome and Islam made a treaty. By this time, the Vatican had obtained an enormous amount of artifacts, knowledge and riches. The Knights Templar posed as the army of God with crosses symbolizing Jesus. They justified their actions by using Jesus Christ as their face. Almost all of the scrolls, books, artifacts, and riches they accumulated was brought back to Rome and stored in the Vatican.

**2 Chronicles 36:18** says, "And all the vessels of the house of God, great and small, and the treasures of the house of the Lord, and the treasures of the king, and of his princes; all these he brought to Babylon."

**After a while some of the Knights Templar figured they should keep the riches for themselves instead of taking everything to the King. The Knights Templar broke off into separate groups to accommodate their own self-interest, and secular agendas**. That's the way the mob operates. They separate and form their own crews. It's not personal, it's just business. However, they have to work together to insure security, and they are all protected by the Vatican. The Knights Templar formed their own little secret societies, and the secret societies of today is simply a continuation of the Knights Templar agenda. They are hooked up with the big bankers, so they have the funding to push their world domination agenda. They all wanted power and wealth, but the most important thing was security and survival. For this they were all forced to compromise with the Roman government, which we know today as the Vatican. There are many secret societies today and they all go back to the Roman Empire. Every aspect of our society is influenced by secret societies. They don't agree with each other 100% of the time, but they all are one with the Vatican. Like they say, **"All roads lead to Rome." But there is only one road to the truth. The truth is Jesus, and the truth will set you free.**

The Roman government merged Christianity in with the pagan religions. Jesus wasn't born on December 25. December 25 is for the winter solstice. **The Christmas tree represents the evergreen trees that people sacrificed and killed their children under to pagan gods. They also decorated those trees, and put Idols under them. Santa is Satan, they just took the 'N' and put it in the middle of the word. The reindeers symbolize the fallen angels. Christmas is all about letting Satan into your house with material possessions.**

**Easter is in respect to the goddess Ishtar.** Ishtar was the Babylonian goddess of fertility and sex. The bunny rabbit is a fertile animal. Eggs come from serpents, snakes, or reptiles. Serpents are demons, and reptiles are serpents.

**Halloween is simply the Devil's holiday.** People dress up as fallen angels and demons. Anything that is half human and half animal is a hybrid. Anything that is half human and half object is a hybrid. Hybrids don't have human DNA. Costumes symbolize demonic possession. Demonic possession corrupts DNA. Anything that has corrupt DNA is outside of the book of life.

As innocent and harmless as St. Valentine's Day may appear, its traditions and customs originate from two of the most sexually perverted pagan festivals of ancient history: Lupercalia and the feast day of Juno Februata. Celebrated on February 15, Lupercalia (known as the "festival of sexual license") was held by the ancient Romans in honor of Lupercus, god of fertility and husbandry, protector of herds and crops, and a mighty hunter—especially of wolves. The Romans believed that Lupercus would protect Rome from roving bands of wolves, which devoured livestock and people. Valentine comes from the Latin Valentinus, which derives from valens, which means "to be strong, powerful, and mighty." The Bible describes a man with a similar title: **Genesis 10:8-9 says, "And Cush begat Nimrod: he began to be a mighty one in the earth. He was a mighty hunter before the Lord: wherefore it is said, Even as Nimrod the mighty hunter before the Lord." However, Nimrod became evil when he came to power and led all of the land into wickedness. Nimrod wanted to kill Abraham. You have to read the book of Jubilees in the Apocrapha to get the details of his life. He was said to have hunted with bow and arrow. Cupid symbolizes Nimrod.**

**The definition of 'Pope' is the 'Vicar of Christ'. 'Vicar of Christ' means that he is in control of the earth instead of Jesus.** Catholicism was established to control the message and gospel of the Bible. They made images of God and angels, then changed the Sabbath day from Saturday to Sunday. Saturday is supposed to be called the 7$^{th}$ day of the week. Days are named by numbers, the names for days today are actually pagan gods. They tried to keep the Bible from being translated from Latin so that the people couldn't know what the Bible actually said. The people could only believe what the Pope or priest said. This is what brought about the Dark Ages. The Dark Ages brought about the Protestant movement. Protestant simply means protesting against Catholicism to serve God outside of Catholicism. **Denominations look like abominations. The Bible is truth. Religion is corrupt. The sons of God are led by the spirit of God.** The Knights Templar performed homosexual rituals, and this is the tradition that is continued today. **They wore skinny paints to show the physique of their legs. Tight paints on men are simply a homosexual tradition common in Europe.** In southern lands people preferred loose clothing so they could get a breeze from the wind. This is why most black men prefer loose clothing and hate cold weather. Tight clothing was mostly worn in northern lands to insulate the body and stay warm.

**Romans 3:4** says, "God forbid: yea, let God be true, but every man a liar; as it is written, That thou mightest be justified in thy sayings, and mightest overcome when thou art judged."

**Matthew 12:25** says, "And Jesus knew their thoughts, and said unto them, "Every kingdom divided against itself is brought to desolation; and every city or house divided against itself shall not stand."

**The Roman government knew that in order to take over the world they needed a support system within their own people. This is why they painted all the people in the Bible white. If white people knew that everyone in the Bible was black, Rome wouldn't have had the support of white people to kill, enslave, and oppress black people. There is no power without land, and the black man had all the good land.** The Vatican and the Pope always knew that Jesus was black. The other secret is that they take orders from the Devil himself. The Devil only has as much power as God allows him to have. Remember, the moon looks like it produces light, but it gets its light from the sun. Their goal is to rule the world and they can't accomplish their goal unless they can keep the black man powerless and strip the resources from the land. They can only get help from their own people or persuade melanated people to kill themselves. Their main concern is to keep people confused about race. Racism is the biggest tool for the power elite. Freemasonry is Knights Templar under a different name. The Nazi movement was to create a pure white race. **The Nazi movement was just a campaign to create a superior race merging blond hair-blue eyed people with demonic DNA. The 'KKK' was a Nazi and masonic organization.** The Nazis succeeded in creating the illusion that white people had a reason to hate melanated people. **The main goal was to make the image of black people look so bad, that people would never consider that Jesus was a black man. If people found that out, their power to oppress black people wouldn't have had as much support.**

**After they ran the Israelites out of Israel, Rome and powers in Europe stayed in a continuous state of stealing and killing. They began their quest to take over the world through deceit. Rothschild made a bargain to have the land of Israel if he could help them win the war at that time by bringing America into it. By bringing America into the war with the Hegelian Dialect, or false flag attack ( problem, reaction, solution), they won the war. Rothschild then funded a migration of Khazars to inhabit the land of Israel.** Rothschild is a Khazar and the Khazars adopted the Hebrew heritage by deceit. It was a benefit for people of white descent to claim the land so that people will believe that Jews were white. This way anyone can be a Jew that is white. Now-a-days people can take a Jewish class to learn the tradition then somehow claim to be a Jew from the tribe of Judah. This way the powers that be can claim Jewish descent to give cover for their wickedness. The Zionist movement is political. They also wanted to control the land between Africa and Asia. **By controlling Israel, they could have a base to control the Middle East and Egypt. The Vatican, Federal Reserve bank in England, State of Israel, and the American military are the forces that the powers use to control the world.**

**Luke 21:24** says, "<u>And they shall fall by the edge of the sword, and shall be led away captive into all nations: and Jerusalem shall be trodden down of the Gentiles, until the times of the Gentiles be fulfilled.</u>"

**The Nazi scientist created all the diseases that we thought were natural but actually conspired. Operation paper clip is when the Nazi scientist were transferred from Europe to South America.** They specialize in sorcery and germ warfare. The Nazi scientist created Methamphetamine for the german soldiers to fight longer in cold climates without food. They created the formula for most of the harmful drugs we have today. They took the natural healing properties from the herbs, added stuff to make it synthetic so they could patent medication and make money from it. They also use technology imparted to them by the fallen angels, and other devices to control the population. **The system of power and control started in ancient Sumer.** Ancient Egypt adopted the system of power and control from the Sumerians, which is symbolized by the pyramid. The pyramid shows that only a few people at the top holds the knowledge while the masses of the people on the bottom remain ignorant. That's how power is maintained. Then Rome adopted that system of power and control, and the evidence of this fact is clearly seen today. All of this knowledge has been preserved and passed down from the fallen angels, Empire to Empire to continue the agenda of the Devil. They use the banking system and stock market of ancient Rome to control the wealth, and keep us in a buying frenzy and constant state of survival. All to keep the economy going and people distracted from what's really going on. Sports is nothing but the Roman Coliseum. They put strong men into competition with each other to restrict them from being a treat to the status quo. Sports are a distraction. Every aspect of our society has been implemented by the modern day Knights Templar. **They don't care about white people no more than they care about black people. They just understand that they need the support of white people to accomplish their goal of world domination.**

**2 Esdras 6:7-9**

**Then answered I and said, what shall be the parting asunder of the times? or when shall be the end of the first, and the beginning of it that followeth?**

**And he said unto me, From Abraham unto Isaac, when Jacob and Esau were born of him, Jacob's hand held first the heel of Esau.**

**For Esau is the end of the world, and Jacob is the beginning of it that followeth.**

**Evil didn't start with the white man. Evil started with the black man in Africa.** Asians and Native Americans are just black people that migrated from Africa. Ancient Egypt was all black people, and the pharaohs used demonic powers to maintain control and influence. It was the African spiritual system of witchcraft taught by the fallen angels that has the world in the trouble we are in today. Europeans were always pagan but they adopted the more sophisticated spiritual system of the Egyptians. **The black man civilized the white man. Europeans drove the black man out of Europe as much as they could to maintain genetic survival. If black and white people breed together the white genotype would become extinct. Black can produce white, but white can't produce black. Albinos are the evidence of this.**

**The demonic agenda today is protected and influenced by the Vatican and the Catholic Church.** The black Pope is the general of the Jesuits. The Jesuits protect the Pope. The Jesuits are the most wicked organization that protects the Devil's agenda. Most Catholics are totally oblivious to what's going on. This is why it is a secret society profoundly specializing in discretion and deceit. Everything God does is in the light. Everything the Devil does is in darkness. **If the light is shown on the Devil, all of his lies and corruption will be exposed. That's why he needs secret societies.** Definition of occult means 'hidden'.

**Revelation 2:9** says, "I know thy works, and tribulation, and poverty, (but thou art rich) and I know the blasphemy of them which say they are Jews, and are not, but are the synagogue of Satan."

# MYSTERY OF THE WHITE MAN & THE BLACK MAN

## ***SHEEP ARE MAINLY BLACK AND WHITE***

## ***GOD STARTED RACE AND SEGREGATION***

## ***FIRST SHALL BE LAST & LAST SHALL BE FIRST***

**Ecclesiastes 3:10-17 says,** "I have seen the travail, which God hath given to the sons of men to be exercised in it.

11. "He hath made every thing beautiful in his time: also he hath set the world in their heart, so that no man can find out the work that God maketh from the beginning to the end.

12. I know that there is no good in them, but for a man to rejoice, and to do good in his life.

13. And also that every man should eat and drink, and enjoy the good of all his labour, it is the gift of God.

14. I know that, whatsoever God doeth, it shall be for ever: nothing can be put to it, nor any thing taken from it: and God doeth it, that men should fear before him.

15. That which hath been is now; and that which is to be hath already been; and God requireth that which is past.

16. And moreover I saw under the sun the place of judgment, that wickedness was there; and the place of righteousness, that iniquity was there.

17. I said in mine heart, God shall judge the righteous and the wicked: for there is a time there for every purpose and for every work."

**What I am going to reveal to you is something that most of you have never considered before. I believe that God has held this understanding back from the world, so his will can be done, for such a time as this. The Devil is trying to start a race war, and if you don't have this understanding you will be deceived. You will go against you own interest in ignorance.**

**Isaiah 42:16** says, **"**And I will bring the blind by a way that they knew not; I will lead them in paths that they have not known: I will make darkness light before them, and crooked things straight." These things will I do unto them, and not forsake them."

**Daniel 12:4** says, "But thou, O Daniel, shut up the words, and seal the book, even to the time of the end: many shall run to and fro, and knowledge shall be increased."

**Matthew 20:16** says, "So the last shall be first, and the first last: for many be called, but few chosen."

Understanding this prophesy will help you realize that the Bible is truly God's word. Paul said, "Covet earnestly the best gifts: and yet shew I unto you a more excellent way." The best gift is prophesy. Prophesy gives confirmation to the truth. If God set something in motion to happen thousands of years before, and it actually happened the way he said it would, then you have to believe that God is all powerful. There are many people who need answers for things they don't understand. This is the understanding to edify God's sheep. God wants us to know certain things in these last days so that our faith can be unmovable.

This is Gods will to strip pride from the hearts of man. In this day and time, it is necessary for people to know the truth because it makes us humble. Only by humility and the fear of the Lord can we be what we were made to be. God wants us to take our eyes off of ourselves and know that he is in control. Pride was the first sin found in Lucifer. If you feel offended by the truth, you have pride in your heart. In order for us to really judge each other by the content of our character, instead of by the color of our skin, we have to have this understanding. God's will is God's will. Everything God does is his business, and we don't have the power to add or take away from it."

## ONLY 2 MAIN COLORS FOR SHEEP: BLACK & WHITE

**The mystery of the white man vs. the black man is found in Genesis 4, and think about verse 15...Numbers 12:10... 2 Kings 5:27... 2 Kings 7:3...Exodus 4:6-7... 2 Chronicles 26...Leviticus chapter 13 & 14. Everything God did wasn't documented, but he's the same yesterday, today, and forever.** Then read **1 Corinthians 1:27**. He who has wisdom will understand the mystery. The mystery is about pride. Pride is what God is trying to remove from the hearts of all men. The only way one can reject the true understanding of this mystery, is if one has pride. Then read **Psalm 10:2-4.** Then read **Isaiah 23:9**. Then read **Proverbs 11:2 & 8:13.** Then read **Daniel 4:37.** Then read **Job 33:17-18.** Then read **Obadiah 1:3.** Then read **1 Timothy 3:6. Get knowledge, get wisdom, and in all your getting, get understanding.**

**Pride was the first sin.** Pride was found in Lucifer, then Eve. After Eve, pride infiltrated mankind. Cain, Miriam, Gehazi, Uzziah, were examples in the bible of people God immediately turned their complexion white because of their pride. The curses on earth that sin produced, first originated from the pride in a black man. **We all have to die, till the ground, menstrual cycles, and painful child birth because of sin that first occurred from a black man.** It was prideful black men that God turned into lepers or albinos. Albinos today are called Lepers in the Bible. Albinos or lepers have no pigment whatsoever, and are the original white people. Evolution is actually albinos (lepers) and Edomites (Neanderthals) evolving into the white people of today. White skin is the physical symbolism of pride. The lepers or albinos and Edomites grew in population to become 'Barbarians'. Barbarians evolved into the white people we know today. Albinos or Lepers are the physical manifestation, and symbolism of pride on earth.

**Numbers 12:10** says, "<u>And the cloud departed from off the tabernacle; and, behold, Miriam became leprous, white as snow: and Aaron looked upon Miriam, and, behold, she was leprous.</u>" **Miriam was Moses sister that had pride against Moses because he married outside of his Hebrew heritage to an Ethiopian woman, and insisted that God should speak to them along with Moses, as if to say Moses wasn't good enough. God became angry at the audacity of her to conspire against his servant Moses and turned her white. Verse 13** says, "And Moses cried unto the Lord, saying, Heal her now, O God, I beseech thee." Then **Verse 14** says, "<u>And the Lord said unto Moses, If her father had but spit in her face, should she not be ashamed seven days? Let her be shut out from the camp seven days, and after that let her be received in again.</u>" **Verse 15** says, "<u>And Miriam was shut out from the camp seven days: and the people journeyed not till Miriam was brought in again.</u>"

**As in Leviticus chapters 13 and 14, everyone that had leprosy was separated from everyone else until they were healed.** White skin was always tied to those that were leprous. Disease was always tied to those that were leprous. **Segregation (separation) was always a result. Dr. King fought for desegregation, and before he died, he said that he was affraid that he had led the people into a burning house.**

**Genesis 4 is the account that lays out the understanding of what happened to people that inherited the curse of Leprosy.** When God cursed Adam and Eve, those curses were for the entire human race. When God cursed Cain, the consequences listed, were for everyone that inherited that particular curse. There were lepers or albinos before the flood and after the flood. God's purpose for this curse was to raise up a nation of white people to do his will in the last days. **God's will is to kill the pride in all mankind for us to repent and fear before him. Cain had pride against God, and was the first documented man that obtained a curse as a visible mark.**

**Genesis 4:11** says, "<u>And now art thou cursed from the earth.</u>"

***Man was created from dust. Dust is dirt. Dirt is soil. Rich soil is black soil. When all the nutrients is stripped from the soil, it becomes lighter in color and calcifies. The correlation for minerals is melanin. The minerals were stripped from the soil Cain was created from, therefore being 'cursed from the earth'. The nutrients and vitamins in our body helps fight disease, so that's why lepers were always white and prone to disease. The disease was leprosy. I believe that leprosy is a primitive term for herpes.***

**Genesis 4:14** says, "Behold, thou hast driven me out this day from the face of the earth; and from thy face shall I be hid; and I shall be a fugitive and a vagabond in the earth; and it shall come to pass, that every one that findeth me shall slay me."

Since everyone else was black, Cain's life was in danger because some people would try to kill him. People would know that he was cursed, and they wouldn't want that curse in their genetics or influence in their society. For this reason those that were lepers or albinos had to separate and head north to the land of Europe or Russia to get away from the melanated people that may want to kill them.

"From thy face shall I be hid" means that Cain's pineal gland became calcified. The pineal gland is the spiritual component in our brains that we connect to God with. When we close our eyes we began to see with the pineal gland. Thats why it is called the third eye. Dreams and visions come via the pineal gland. The pineal gland is also responsible for rhythm and coordination. It helps the immune system, helps block radiation, and it's activated in darkness. That's why you close your eyes when you meditate and get sleepy when the lights are off. Some white men today have more since than most black men. However, the only way certain white men could have committed the terrorism they have on earth, chase wild animals, and jump out of airplanes for fun is because there is a void in the pineal gland. It's hard for them to hear God saying, "Stop! What you're doing is deadly and not worth the thrill."

**Genesis 4:12** says, "When thou tillest the ground, it shall not henceforth yield unto thee her strength; a fugitive and a vagabond shalt thou be in the earth."

There are very few fruit or herbs native to Europe or Russia. Albinos can't till the ground efficiently in the daytime because of skin cancer from sun burn. Most of the herbs (medicine) and spices that Europe and Russia obtained came from other lands. The land of Europe and Russia does not yield its strength.

**Genesis 4:15** says, "And the Lord said unto him, Therefore whosoever slayeth Cain, vengeance shall be taken on him sevenfold. And the Lord set a mark upon Cain, lest any finding him should kill him."

Cain was already cursed to live a miserable life. If God wanted him dead, he would have killed him. God had a purpose for the future generations of the lepers or albinos, so God made a way for them to populate by separating them from black people.

However, black men had killed many white men (lepers) since the beginning of time, and in the last 400 years the white man turned around to take vengeance on the black man sevenfold, just like God said would happen. The white man created the gun, and it has resulted in seven times more black deaths than white deaths since the beginning of time. God allowed the white man to populate to later put the white man in power to fulfill the prophecy, 'The first shall be last, and the last shall be first.' Also, to show all man what happens when pride rules the world. The black man ruled the world first, then the black man sunk to the bottom of society. If this is a white man's world now, and white skin symbolizes pride, then the world is ran by pride. We now see the results of what pride has done. God wants everyone to learn from this and to humble ourselves before him, for by humility is the only way we can be what God created us to be.

**Ecclesiastes 3:14** says, "I know that, whatsoever God doeth, it shall be for ever: nothing can be put to it, nor any thing taken from it: and God doeth it, that men should fear before him."

**In Genesis 1:1-5, God said, "Let there be light" when it was only darkness. God let there be white men when it was only black men. God saw that the light was good, so the white man is good for the will of God.** The will of God is the only thing that's important. God uses his creation to teach us a lesson. We reap what we sow. God wants us to wake up and be humble. No matter who you are, pride is what will destroy you. **The white man is not pride, but only symbolism of pride, because it took pride to turn a black man white. Those that were white were separated from the rest of the black people as a punishment for their pride. In the last 400 years, those who were black were separated from white people as a punishment for their pride. What goes around comes around. The first shall be last, and the last shall be first.**

**Albinos or lepers, since the beginning of time, were always getting killed in Africa, so they migrated north to get away from danger. People didn't migrate to cold climates, where the land doesn't yield its strength, for fun. They did so for safety and survival, and to avoid sun burn.**

**In some places in Africa today they have communities outside of cities that protect Albino children from anyone that may want to kill them. The black people in Africa that prey on albinos today are the wicked people that sacrifice albinos to demons for spiritual powers. This foolishness has been going on since the beginning, and this is the reason black people kill each other and will never get reparations. Black people**

**inherited the curse for what their ancestors have been doing to white people since the beginning of time. "Therefore whosoever slayeth Cain, vengeance shall be taken on him sevenfold."** God wants us to see how all is vanity, and how humility is the key. We have to make ourselves last as a servant if we want to be exalted first. Our purpose as God's creation is to serve God. Jesus was the example of a servant.

**1 Corinthians 1:27** says, "But God hath chosen the foolish things of the world to confound the wise; and God hath chosen the weak things of the world to confound the things which are mighty."

**Ecclesiastes 7:13** says, "Consider the work of God: for who can make that straight, which he hath made crooked?

**White people would have never supported the vengeance and affliction on black people if they knew Jesus was black**. However, a curse came upon Israel because they rejected Jesus and chose Barabbas.

**Matthew 27:20** says, "**But the chief priests and elders persuaded the multitude that they should ask Barabbas, and destroy Jesus**."

It was already ordained that vengeance be taken on the black man sevenfold for killing lepers, so a great dillusion was set up to fulfill prophecy. This is why Rome needed paintings of white people posing as Hebrews. Imagery is powerful, and that's why God said not to make any images of him because people believe what they see. The white man has been a victim of deceit just as much as the black man. Europeans were decieved into believing Jesus was white and black people were savages in order to willfully kill them without concious. Pride is always the factor that makes a man comfortable with evil. **God used the pride in the white man to kill the pride in the black man. Then he used the knowledge and understanding of truth in the black man to kill the pride in the white man.**

Obadiah 1:6 says "How are the things of Esau searched out! how are his hidden things sought up!

7. All the men of thy confederacy have brought thee even to the border: the men that were at peace with thee have deceived thee, and prevailed against thee; they that eat thy bread have laid a wound under thee: there is none understanding in him.

8. Shall I not in that day, saith the LORD, even destroy the wise men out of Edom, and understanding out of the mount of Esau?"

However, God allowed prophecy to take place in order for people to fear him. God didn't allow the translators to corrupt his word, all they did was change names to fit an Edomite image. **God said he was going to give himself and his people's heritage to the heathen as in Psalm 111:6. Joel 2:17 bears witness.** Jesus took on a gentile name just like the Hebrew slaves took on a gentile name. Jesus hung from a tree just like the Hebrew slaves hung from a tree. God went through the same things his people went through to leave a sign for the world to see. **He also let the white man spread the gospel all over the world to show man that he has no respect of persons.**

**Ephesians 2:8-9** says, **"For by grace are ye saed through faith; and that not of yourselves: it is the gift of God: 9. Not of works, lest any man should boast."**

God works in those that are broken and hungry for truth. Not in those that are spoiled and prideful. Jesus is the way, truth and life.

The Europeans (gentiles) didn't have natural resources on the land, so scarcity caused them to explore other lands. Without the exploration from desperation, the Europeans wouldn't have spread the gospel of Jesus Christ all over the world. They took books out, replaced words in certain translations, but the King James version is the version that God allowed to be legit. Much knowledge was intentionaly hid from man allowed by God until the last days. Jesus was rejected by his own people, moreover the 12 tribes of Israel had to fulfill the prophetic curses of breaking the covenant in Deuteronomy 28.

**If the white man manipulated the Bible for a tool to oppress black people, then the Bible would have had God cursing people 'black as the ground', instead of, 'white as snow'. Those that believe that the Bible was written by the white man are simply making conclusions on what was said about the Bible instead of what it actually says.**

God allowed the righteous man Job to be afflicted by the devil. We all have to be tested in forgiveness. Jesus forgave his killers. To love your enemies is the test of persecution. We don't wrestle against flesh and blood. The Powers, principalities, wickedness in high places and the rulers of the darkness of this age are the real enemy. The evil spirits in the Europeans controlled them to commit all the terrorism on Israel and everyone else. Now we see Israel has become brainwashed and the demons in the people have us killing each other. Satan wants everyone to be in hell with him. God gave us all an opportunity to forgive so we may be forgiven. Satan wants people to be unforgiving to disqualify man for forgiveness. God allows all man to eat the fruit of our own doings. However, all things work together for good to those who love God and who are called according to his purpose.

Cain and Abel, Ishmael and Issac, and Jacob and Esau are brother pairs that show opposites. One brother is blessed and the other brother is cursed. Cain, Ishmael, and Esau are cursed. Cain was marked with white skin like Michael Jackson. Esau was born a redneck and hairy all over as a neanderthal. Ishmael was black, but the Ishmaelites mixed with Esau during the Ottoman Empire and became the lightskin Arabians we know today. Each of these cursed brothers were the first born son. Abel, Issac, and Jacob are blessed. Each of these blessed brothers were born second. Being born first symbolizes power over the second born son in this life. When Jesus comes back, he will put the second born son in power over the first born son and the entire earth. The first born son Ishmael started Islam, and the firstborn son Esau are Romans, Khazars, and rednecks all over the world that love pride and hate Jacob (Israel).

**Romans 9:17** says, "For the scripture saith unto Pharaoh, Even for this same purpose have I raised thee up, that I might shew my power in thee, and that my name might be declared throughout all the earth."

**Romans 9:18** says, "Therefore hath he mercy on whom he will have mercy, and whom he will he hardeneth."

**Romans 9:15** says, "For he saith to Moses, I will have mercy on whom I will have mercy, and I will have compassion on whom I will have compassion."

**Ecclesiastes 4:1** says, "So I returned, and considered all the oppressions that are done under the sun: and behold the tears of such as were oppressed, and they had no comforter; and on the side of their oppressors there was power; but they had no comforter." (The Holy Ghost is the comforter.)

This was Gods will to strip pride from the hearts of man. In this day and time, it is necessary for people to know the truth because it makes everyone humble. Only by humility and the fear of the Lord can we be what we were made to be. If you feel offended by the truth, you have pride in your heart. In order for us to really judge each other by the content of our character, instead of by the color of our skin, we have to have this understanding. All wisdom and knowledge comes from God. Outside the viewpoint of the most high, you're in a delusion. There is a way that seems right to a man, but the end is destruction. God's thoughts are not our thoughts, neither his ways our ways. He who has an ear, let him hear what the spirit of the Lord is saying to the Saints. The Bible is the only book that gives the understanding of why there is black and white people on the Earth. This is a witness to the fact that the Bible is the true word of prophesy.

**Acts 28:27 says, "For the heart of this people is waxed gross, and their ears are dull of hearing, and their eyes have they closed; lest they should see with their eyes, and hear with their ears, and understand with their heart, and should be converted, and I should heal them."**

*****FIRST SHALL BE LAST & LAST SHALL BE FIRST*****

# GOD GAVE THE GOSPEL TO THE GENTILES

**Acts 13:46** says, "Then Paul and Barnabas waxed bold, and said, it was necessary that the word of God should first have been spoken to you: but seeing ye put it from you, and judge yourselves unworthy of everlasting life, lo, we turn to the Gentiles." **God knew that the real Jews couldn't resist the pagan influence of the world and they wouldn't successfully spread the gospel of Jesus to the world because of pride, political, and religious strongholds.** They were afraid of losing their life, businesses, and religious institutions to the Roman authority, and Pharisees that were supported by Rome. Obeying the gospel of Jesus Christ was knew and contradicted the religious system that existed, which would have put the Pharises out of business. Therefore, God raised up the gentiles to spread the gospel to the four corners of the earth. Also to fulfill prophecy, **"Last shall be first."**

The way they were then, we act the same way now with the cares of the world through religious compromise, and politics. **There are preachers who won't tell the whole truth, because they are scared of being different, and fear losing their audience.** Most preachers just want to maintain the money that they bring in by speaking a feel good message. Powers that be still try to regulate and limit the message taught in churches. We are still indoctrinated by demonic deceit by all religions. **The Bible is not a religion. The Bible is truth. Bible schools teach religion, and how to build a mega church, but Jesus taught truth. Jesus didn't allow money exchange in the temple, for he said it will be called the house of prayer. James 1:27** says,

"Pure religion, and undefiled before God and the Father is this, to visit the fatherless and widows in their affliction, and to keep himself unspotted from the world."

**An inherited sin for one person, may be a sin that another person opens a door to. We were all born in sin, so no one can condemn a person for sin. However, God has called us all to correction and reproof.** We can't be perfect in our flesh. That's why we are saved by grace. **Trying to be perfect in the flesh without considering God's grace, leaves you with the impression that you can earn your way into heaven.** If man could earn their way into Heaven, then Jesus' sacrifice wouldn't have been necessary for us to have the Holy Spirit. Repentance and the Holy Spirit keeps our DNA from being defilled. **Ephesians 2:9** says, "For by grace are ye saved through faith; and that not of yourselves: it is the gift of God. Not of works, lest any man should boast." The Jews were caught up in keeping the law, and trying to earn salvation, but they were lousy law keepers. Man can't keep the law. Only by the assistance of the Holy Ghost can man keep the law, so that would be God in us keeping his own law. **God knew the Europeans were hungry for truth, and God chose them to spread the Bible all over the world. What was said about the Bible is where the deception comes in. Moreover, having the scriptures in tangible form so we can read it ourselves is the real blessing. Thats God's grace and mercy upon all flesh that we may be saved in these last and evil days.**

**Romans chapter 11:**

**1. "I say then, Hath God cast away his people? God forbid. For I also am an Israelite, of the seed of Abraham, of the tribe of Benjamin.**

**2. God hath not cast away his people which he foreknew. Wot ye not what the scripture saith of Elias? how he maketh intercession to God against Israel, saying,**

**3. Lord, they have killed thy prophets, and digged down thine altars; and I am left alone, and they seek my life.**

**4. But what saith the answer of God unto him? I have reserved to myself seven thousand men, who have not bowed the knee to the image of Baal.**

**5. Even so then at this present time also there is a remnant according to the election of grace.**

**6. And if by grace, then is it no more of works: otherwise grace is no more grace. But if it be of works, then is it no more grace: otherwise work is no more work.**

**7. What then? Israel hath not obtained that which he seeketh for; but the election hath obtained it, and the rest were blinded**

**8. (According as it is written, God hath given them the spirit of slumber, eyes that they should not see, and ears that they should not hear;) unto this day.**

**9. And David saith, Let their table be made a snare, and a trap, and a stumblingblock, and a recompence unto them:**

**10. Let their eyes be darkened, that they may not see, and bow down their back alway.**

**11. I say then, Have they stumbled that they should fall? God forbid: but rather through their fall**

**salvation is come unto the Gentiles, for to provoke them to jealousy.**

**12. Now if the fall of them be the riches of the world, and the diminishing of them the riches of the Gentiles; how much more their fulness?**

**13. For I speak to you Gentiles, inasmuch as I am the apostle of the Gentiles, I magnify mine office:**

**14. If by any means I may provoke to emulation them which are my flesh, and might save some of them.**

**15. For if the casting away of them be the reconciling of the world, what shall the receiving of them be, but life from the dead?**

**16. For if the firstfruit be holy, the lump is also holy: and if the root be holy, so are the branches.**

**17. And if some of the branches be broken off, and thou, being a wild olive tree, wert graffed in among them, and with them partakest of the root and fatness of the olive tree;**

**18. Boast not against the branches. But if thou boast, thou bearest not the root, but the root thee.**

**19. Thou wilt say then, The branches were broken off, that I might be graffed in.**

**20. Well; because of unbelief they were broken off, and thou standest by faith. Be not highminded, but fear:**

**21. For if God spared not the natural branches, take heed lest he also spare not thee.**

**22. Behold therefore the goodness and severity of God: on them which fell, severity; but toward thee, goodness, if thou continue in his goodness: otherwise thou also shalt be cut off.**

**23. And they also, if they abide not still in unbelief, shall be graffed in: for God is able to graff them in again.**

**24. For if thou wert cut out of the olive tree which is wild by nature, and wert graffed contrary to nature into a good olive tree: how much more shall these, which be the natural branches, be graffed into their own olive tree?**

**25. For I would not, brethren, that ye should be ignorant of this mystery, lest ye should be wise in your own conceits; that blindness in part is happened to Israel, until the fulness of the Gentiles be come in.**

**26. And so all Israel shall be saved: as it is written, There shall come out of Sion the Deliverer, and shall turn away ungodliness from Jacob:**

**27. For this is my covenant unto them, when I shall take away their sins.**

**28. As concerning the gospel, they are enemies for your sakes: but as touching the election, they are beloved for the fathers' sakes.**

**29. For the gifts and calling of God are without repentance.**

**30. For as ye in times past have not believed God, yet have now obtained mercy through their unbelief:**

**31. Even so have these also now not believed, that through your mercy they also may obtain mercy.**

**32. For God hath concluded them all in unbelief, that he might have mercy upon all.**

**33. O the depth of the riches both of the wisdom and knowledge of God! how unsearchable are his judgments, and his ways past finding out!**

**34. For who hath known the mind of the Lord? or who hath been his counsellor?**

**35. Or who hath first given to him, and it shall be recompensed unto him again?**

**36. For of him, and through him, and to him, are all things: to whom be glory for ever. Amen.**

**Any doctrine besides what the Bible teaches is witchcraft.** Trying to keep the law and being perfect is righteousness, but once you break one law, it's as if you broke all the laws. Without the shedding of blood there is no remission of sin. **Matthew 26:28** says, "For this is my blood of the new testament, which is shed for many for the remission of sins." Jesus died so that we can be redeemed from the curse of the law. Now we are saved by grace. Trying to be perfect without Jesus is the spirit of Anti-Christ, because man always finds a way to cheat and justify his actions that are contrary to the will of God.

Proverbs 16:2 says, "All the ways of a man are clean in his own eyes; but the Lord weigheth the spirits."

**Commit your works unto the Lord, and your thoughts will be established. You can't get perfect and then decide to serve the Lord. Decide to serve the Lord, then the Lord will work righteousness in you. We get rid of bad habits by picking up good habits.** Read **Galatians**. From the law to grace, from Adam to Jesus, from Abraham to Paul, from Ishmael to Isaac from black to white, from Jew to Gentile, from Egypt to America. That's why you have to read the Bible yourself, to know for yourself, so you may not be deceived.

**Acts 13:48** says, "And when the Gentiles heard this, they were glad, and glorified the word of the Lord: and as many as were ordained to eternal life believed." This means that a preacher can be filled with the Holy Ghost and do all he can to lead people to Jesus, but if a person is not ordained to eternal life, chances are he/she won't truly believe. God has to help us believe. **We can't really believe unless God ordains us to believe. Those who truly believe are blessed.**

# PROOF THAT THE (KJV) BIBLE IS THE ONLY WORD FOR SALVATION

**1 John 4** says, "Beloved, believe not every spirit, but try the spirits whether they are of God: because many false prophets are gone out into the world. Hereby know ye the Spirit of God: Every spirit that confesseth that Jesus Christ is come in the flesh is of God: And every spirit that confesseth not that Jesus Christ is come in the flesh is not of God: and this is that spirit of antichrist, whereof ye have heard that it should come; and even now already is it in the world."

**Charles Tayes Russell was a freemason that started the Jehovah's Witness cult and Joseph Smith was a freemason that started the Mormon cult.** They are both a diversion from the Bible to exploit and extract money from the people. The King James Version Bible is the only truth. Praying to the dead and doing rituals was the structure of these early beginnings. When it was popular, they taught that black people didn't have a soul. The Mormon belief is so crazy, I don't understand how anyone can even consider it. It's so out there, I don't want to talk about it. When they originated they used symbols from the Masonic lodge. These cults teach another gospel than what the Bible teaches. The spirit of deception and confusion. Witchcraft with a Christian face. The Mormons believe Joseph Smith's private interpretation that he got by the way of magic. It's said that he put his face in a hat within some magical seer stone and glasses. Then by channeling a spirit, he received another gospel that he had someone write down as he spoke. **Galatians 1:9** says, "As we said before, so say I now again, if any man preach any other gospel unto you than that ye have received, let him be accursed." Joseph Smith had his followers to wear magical undergarments that has some logo that is said to brand an imprint in the skin when you wear them. **Magical under pants!!!** When you think you've heard it all…

**It's a given that magic is sorcery and witchcraft.** You remember the McDonalds commercial. "Do you believe in Magic? And I hope you do, you'll always have a friend wearing big red shoes." Ronald McDonald clown of McDonalds indoctrinating kids into witchcraft deceitfully. There is a demon witches identify with that looks like a clown. We've accepted clowns as entertainment for kids. **Harry Potter is a book that subtly teaches kids sorcery and how to conjure and communicate with demonic spirits.** This is what America has become. Cartoons, action figures, and superheroes like superman, batman, and Spiderman which symbolize giants or Nephilim, and Fallen Angels. Talking animals with human characteristics. Angels in heaven are a more advanced creation, but have likeness of the animals on Earth. The fallen angels made offspring with human women that had man and animal-like characteristics. Hollywood has people with animal characteristics of various kinds, having spiritual powers like Marvel heroes and cartoons.

**The Holly tree was a tree the ancient druids was said to make magic wands out of. They say the Holly Tree has certain magical powers. Magic is witchcraft, and Hollywood is so called for respect of the Holly Tree.** By the way of Hollywood, people are hypnotized, spiritually manipulated, deceived by imagery, desensitized, and coerced into all types of foolishness. **The fallen angels are in a different dimension that can only cross over through portals, and those are the demons people are deceived into thinking they're aliens.** Demons can only do what they have legal right to do. These are the demons that people open the door to be possessed with when they go into transcendental meditation, and try to astral project and levitate. These are the demons that people encounter when they think they've been abducted by aliens. **The more blood sacrifices and demonic rituals that are done open up doors for powerful demons to enter our dimension.** The more sin that's on earth means more demons will be among us. **Hollywood is the catalyst that desensitizes the world to demons.**

**Ephesians 3:18** says, "May be able to comprehend with all saints what is the breadth, and length, and depth, and height."

**Proverbs 25:3** says, "The heaven for height, and the earth for depth, and the heart of kings is unsearchable."

**Psalm 148:1** says, "Praise ye the Lord. Praise ye the Lord from the heavens: praise him in the heights."

**Job 22:12** says, "Is not God in the height of heaven? and behold the height of the stars, how high they are!"

**Catholicism is witchcraft with a Christian face. Exodus 20:4** says, "Thou shalt not make unto thee any graven image, or any likeness of anything that is in heaven above, or that is in the earth beneath, or that is in the water under the earth." **There are more images of God, angels, etc…in the Catholic Church more so than any other institution in the world. Exodus 20:8** says, "Remember the sabbath day, to keep it holy." **The powers of the Catholic Church deliberately changed the Sabbath day from Saturday to Sunday.** Praying to the Saints like Marry, and Peter is praying to the dead. When Jesus died, and rose by the power of God, he became the high priest, so man can go straight to God with prayer, confession, and repentance, instead of having a man intercede that is unqualified. Jesus is the intercessor. Priest are there to play Jesus, gather information on people to manipulate and control. The Pope is called the Vicar of Christ. This means the whole Earth belongs to the Pope. Every person, all land, water and sky belongs to the Pope. That's blasphemy.

**Allister Crowley, who wrote the 'The Book of the Law,' could communicate with Satan, and said the greatest sacrifice to Satan was to rape an innocent young boy, kill him, then drink his blood.** He was known as the most wicked man on Earth for the hundred plus children he destroyed. This is why Catholic priest molest young boys. Anyone that molests children is doing the work of Satan. In the basement of the Vatican, it's said that they do satanic rituals by killing innocent children and drinking their blood. It's said that the Vatican is responsible for most of the child and sex trafficking consisting mostly of boys. It is also said that the Vatican has a telescope they call 'Lucifer'. The Pope is protected by the Black Pope, which is the general of the Jesuit order. The Jesuits protect the Pope and the occult agenda. It is said that the Jesuits ordered the assassination of JFK and many more. Catholicism and all secret societies stem from the Knights Templar. The mob and mafia is protected by the Catholic Church. They've done a good job of keeping the power in the bloodline. The Jewish state in Israel was politically created, so that Europeans can claim to be Jews and have the religious right to do what they want.

**Revelation 3:9 says, "Behold, I will make them of the synagogue of Satan, which say they are Jews, and are not, but do lie; behold, I will make them to come and worship before thy feet, and to know that I have loved thee."** This is why I have to tell the truth, because Jesus said, "My people are destroyed for the lack of knowledge, if you love me feed my sheep, the truth shall set you free, and for the wrath of God is revealed from heaven against all ungodliness and unrighteousness of men, who hold the truth in unrighteousness. Every belief system besides the Bible teaches deceit. God's word is literal. Some concepts are spiritually discerned. **Without the Holy Ghost, it can be difficult to rightly divide the word of truth.** That's why you have to read it for yourself.

**Work-based salvation is witchcraft.** There are many cults in the world. Gnosticism is salvation through knowledge. The devil has succeeded through a deceitful belief, which preys on pride, called the "Ancient Hope." **The Ancient Hope is an occult belief that man can one day live forever by the use of knowledge, science, and technology.** Science is a distraction to take the glory from God. **Outside the viewpoint of the most high God you're in a delusion. Science test God's creation and make conclusions**. **1 Timothy 6:20** says, "O Timothy, keep that which is committed to thy trust, avoiding profane and vain babblings, and oppositions of science falsely so called: which some professing have erred concerning the faith. Grace be with thee. Amen."

God's word teaches us that Jesus is the only way to eternal life." Moreover, who in the world would want to live forever without the creator anyway? **On Earth things don't get better, they get worse.** Death is a doorway to either separation, or consecration. We are saved by grace through our belief, and if you really believe in Jesus and led by the Holy Spirit, you're going to bear fruit. You will get to work. **Commit your works unto the Lord and your thoughts will be established.** We get delivered by seeking the Lord and committing our works unto him. Why would the Lord poor his blessings into those who are going to sit around and do nothing with it. God has called us to bear good fruit, but we can't bear good fruit without the guidance of the Holy Spirit. Amazing is his grace. Seek and ye shall find. To seek is a sacrifice, and nothing good comes without sacrifice. He who hungers and thirst after righteousness shall be filled. **James 4:8 says**, "Draw nigh to God, and he will draw nigh to you. Cleanse your hands, ye sinners; and purify your hearts, ye double minded." **James 4:10** says, "Humble yourselves in the sight of the Lord, and he shall lift you up." This is the instruction, and for those that take heed, **Proverbs 8:35** says, "For whoso findeth me findeth life, and shall obtain favour of the Lord." Pray and meditate on the Holy Spirit. **God speaks through his word, so we have to know his word to discern the Holy Spirit.**

# OUR THOUGHTS INVOKE THE SPIRIT

**The law of attraction is one of God's spiritual laws on earth**. Whatever we meditate on, is what we draw to us. Our thoughts turn into actions and words. Our thoughts are influenced by spirit, and our words are spirit. We give spirits permission to work according to our words. When we curse, we open the door to be cursed. When we bless, we open the door to be blessed. God's word is spirit. The way we think, act, and speak put spirits in motion accordingly. **This is why God told us, in his word, how to think.**

**2 Corinthians 10:5** says "Casting down imaginations, and every high thing that exalteth itself against the knowledge of God, and bringing into captivity every thought to the obedience of Christ." **Philippians 4:8** says "Finally, brethren, whatsoever things are true, whatsoever things are honest, whatsoever things are just, whatsoever things are pure, whatsoever things are lovely, whatsoever things are of good report; if there be any virtue, and if there be any praise, think on these things." **Joshua 1:8** says "This book of the law shall not depart out of thy mouth; but thou shalt meditate therein day and night, that thou mayest observe to do according to all that is written therein: for then thou shalt make thy way prosperous, and then thou shalt have good success." **Psalm 1:2** says "But his delight is in the law of the Lord; and in his law doth he meditate day and night." **Psalm 119:15** says "I will meditate in thy precepts, and have respect unto thy ways."

**It is highly important to discern the Holy Spirit and evil spirits.** There is only one Holy Spirit, but there are many evil spirits. The sun represents Jesus Christ. The sun gives life and light to everything. The moon and stars represent Lucifer and the fallen angels. The moon gets its light from the sun, but can't give life, and only has enough light to make you think it has light. When you meditate you have to meditate on the sun, metaphorically speaking as the almighty God, in order to draw the Holy Spirit, which is light, to you. If you meditate on anything else, you can open yourself up to the devil and the multitude of evil spirits that are out there, like the moon and stars which are in darkness. The moon and stars can appear as the true light, but the moon gets its light from the sun, and you have to be in darkness to see the stars anyway. There is only one truth, the way it is only one sun. **In order to really know God, you have to know his word, so if you encounter any other spirit you can discern if it's from God or not.**

**Psalm 1:1-2** says, "<u>Blessed is the man that walketh not in the counsel of the ungodly, nor standeth in the way of sinners, nor sitteth in the seat of the scornful. But his delight is in the law of the Lord; and in his law doth he meditate day and night.</u>"

# ORIGIN OF ISLAM

In the Old Testament, people had to sacrifice a Lamb or animal God saw acceptable, for the remission of sin. For without the shedding of blood there is no remission of sin. The sacrifice was laid on the alter, and the Priest would go into the Holies of holies to see if God would accept the sacrifice. When Jesus died, the cross was the alter, his body was the sacrifice, and when he rose from the dead he became the high priest. Now we don't have to sacrifice animals anymore for our sins. Jesus became the perfect Lamb of God, as the last blood sacrifice for the remission of sin. **If you believe only the Old Testament is valid, like the Islam religion, but not the New Testament, that only means that you are supposed to continue making animal sacrifices like the Old Testament required.**

The prophet Mahammad of the Muslim religion was said to have been a honest man that had somewhat of a hard life eventually began to search out his purpose and seek spiritual understanding of what life was all about. **He went to a mountain called Jebil Nur and into a cave called Gar Hira for several spiritual retreats concentrated on intense personal reflection and meditation**. He would spend hours, whole days and nights, in intense, fervent meditation. Then one day in 610 AD. something happened. History says that Mahammad was meditating and fell asleep. **Then suddenly he awoke in abject terror. His body was shaking uncontrollably. He said that an angel had him in such a tight suffocating embrace as if it were squeezing the life out of him.** As he laid there completely shattered he heard a voice that said "Read," Mahammad said that he couldn't read. The voice said again "Read", and he again said, "I cannot read", but on the 3rd time he said, "What shall I read?"

**Mahammad ran home to his wife, in terror, and said "Cover me! What has happened to me? I fear for myself." With all of his doubts she was the one who reassured him about his experience. She reconciled him with what had really happened, that he met an angel of God**. But after he came to himself, he was thrown into a complete crisis because of the silence. He was confused and in total despair **almost to the point of suicide.** He was still in doubt to what had happened to him. Then one morning the revelations began again. Mahammad began to realize he had a responsibility**. He believed that God had given him a message.**

Mahammad was later banned from Mecca. In Medina he gained power and constituted peace with the Constitution of Medina that judged each person by their religion. It was a type of freedom of religion but not like today.

**He was said to have astral projected to Jerusalem 800 miles from mecca overnight.** Said that he met Old Testament prophets, got close to the throne of God, and received the 5 prayers a day message. He received a revelation that people in mecca could serve their gods, but was later said that revelation came from Satan and was thrown out. It was said that claim was a lie and not accepted by Muslims.

**Chapter 2 verse 191 & 218 of the Quran, says that persecution is worse than slaughter.** Was said to be an excuse to get revenge on the people that expelled Mahammad from Mecca. **Mahammad received a series of revelations urging him to fight back against those who expelled them from their homes.** Mahammad won the battle at Madr by attacking the trading route from mecca to Syria, bringing back gifts to medina, and giving him more prestige than even before. He compared it to the Israelites deliverance at the Red Sea.

**Then he received a revelation to change the direction of prayer from the direction of Jerusalem to the direction of Mecca, symbolizing a new Identity for the religion.** He claimed the Jews were taking sides with the Quraysh, the army of mecca**, then ordered the death of 800 Jews on the charge of treason.** It was said that he let someone else be the judge. However, **he had banishing 2 other Jewish tribes before.** He had seen off all opposition to his rule and became the most powerful man in all Arabia. **He married to create alliances with tribes in the Arab nation against Mecca.** Later he eventually made peace with the Quraysh of Mecca.

**Allegedlly he revelations that Mahammad received throughout his life is what made up the Quran. Every time he had a revelation it was a terrifying and an exhausting experience.** He frequently had to struggle to make sense of them. Some came as words, and some as visions that needed intense concentration to understand their meaning. Mahammad said, "Never had I received a revelation without feeling that my soul had been torn from my body." He'd go pale, and he'd sweat even on a cold day. He practiced contemplative meditation. **It's one sentence I can sum all of this up with. "THE BEST WAY TO FLOAT A LIE IS ON A BOATLOAD OF TRUTH."**

**The muslims continued their quest for power in Africa and in Europe. The Ottoman Empire was dominant in Europe because the muslims captured the black Jews in Africa and traded them for guns. The black Jews in Africa were compelled to submit to Islam or die. How can God make a prophet outside of Israel to kill and enslave Israel. Makes no sense whatsoever.**

**First of all God chooses prophets for his people from the 12 tribes of Israel (Jacob). Mahammad was an Ishmaelite. Abraham and Sarai had Isaac. Abraham and Hagar, the bondwoman of Sarai, had Ishmael. Isaac was birthed from the promise of God to multiply Abraham's seed. Ishmael was birthed because the lack of belief in the promise. Ishmael was not born by faith, he was born by the law of what the flesh is capable of. Islam is works based salvation.**

# THE HOLY SPIRIT VS. EVIL SPIRITS

**1 John 4** says, "Beloved, believe not every spirit, but try the spirits whether they are of God: because many false prophets are gone out into the world. Hereby know ye the Spirit of God: Every spirit that confesseth that Jesus Christ is come in the flesh is of God: And every spirit that confesseth not that Jesus Christ is come in the flesh is not of God: and this is that spirit of antichrist, whereof ye have heard that it should come; and even now already is it in the world."

**2 Corinthians 11:14** says "And no marvel; for Satan himself is transformed into an angel of light."

**I have been attacked by an evil spirit 3 times before. Every time I was attacked I felt like I was paralyzed, suffocating, and the third time I felt like my soul was being torn from my body**. The first time, I experienced paralysis and suffocation. The second time it was paralysis, suffocation, and it was trying to communicate with me. I heard a whispery technological jibber jabber that sounded like aliens from outter space sending messages to earth that would have to be decoded. The third time I was attacked by a demon, I felt a vast amount of pressure on my pineal gland. I felt all of my body weight leaving as if I was empty space and I began to levitate. Every time I was attacked, I called on Jesus and the evil spirit went away. **If you have sleep paralysis, you are being attacked by an evil spirit. They love to attack people at their weakest point.** Some demons are more powerful than others. Demons telepathically transfer messages to people along the pineal gland, and one has to be possessed in order to receive the message in accuracy. Those that think they were abducted by alien, were actually possessed by demons. Now I understand why people think demons are aliens. They make aliens in movies sound like demons. Hollywood know what demons sound like, and they want to deceive people into thinking that aliens are real and demons aren't. Nasa has been covering this up since the beginning. The plan is to fake an alien invasion in order to give demons permission to run around posing as our saviors that have returned to save man from itself.

**Mahammad was at his weakest point when he first encountered that spirit. He was being suffocated and was also terrified. 2 Timothy 1:7** says "For God hath not given us the spirit of fear; but of power, and of love, and of a sound mind." That's exactly the opposite of what Mahammad experienced. God said meditate on my word day and night, because if you meditate on anything else, you can draw any foul spirit to you and you open yourself up to demonic possession. **Some Asians that do transcendental meditation, to levitate and astral project, are channeling spirits not of God.** Demonic spirits can give you supernatural power, but its moon power and not sun power. God wants us to have faith and to accept what he allows. **Any powers you want to obtain from evil spirits, you have to pay for it with your soul.** The Hindu religion is just like Islam. They believe in meditation, but draw the wrong spirits. **Some spirits are deceitful and make you think they are angels of light.**

**Mahammad was attacked by a demon, and because he ignorantly submitted to it, that demon was able to use Mahammad as his vessel.** Jesus said, "Resist the devil, and he will flee." Jesus also said, "My people are destroyed for the lack of knowledge." **Mahammad was terrified when that demon was communicating with him, however, his wife convinced him he met God, and**

**because of his ignorance, he thought it was an angel of the Most High God.**

I experience the Holy Spirit every day. Every time I feel the Holy Spirit, I get humble, I might cry, and I praise God. Most of the time I start preaching or praying. Most of the time I meditate for direction and comfort. I don't get scared or fearful. The Holy Spirit makes you brave and confident, not confused. **The voice of The Holy Spirit comes along the pineal gland.** If your pineal gland isn't active, it is hard to hear the Holy Spirit. All the poisons in our food and water is to attack the pineal gland so we can't connect with the Holy Spirit. **Prayer and meditation exercises the pineal gland.** The Holy Spirit is a still voice of peace and love that speaks your language. **You have to train yourself to hear God's voice by prayer and meditating on The Word of God.** You can't force thoughts, but let your mind be at peace after you pray and consider all things unto the Lord. Once you learn to hear God's voice, through prayer and meditation, you can then have the mind of Christ. **If you meditate without Jesus on your mind, you can draw any foul spirit to you.** I have surety, because the fruits of the Holy Spirit are love, joy, peace, longsuffering, gentleness, goodness, faith, Meekness, and temperance. That's how to know the spirit of God. We test the Spirits with the Word of God (KJV Bible). **Every Spirit is not of God.**

**2 Corinthians 11:14** says "And no marvel; for Satan himself is transformed into an angel of light." Remember, the moon appears to give light, but it gets its light from the sun.

**Matthew 18:16** and **2 Corinthians 13:1** says, "In the mouth of two or three witnesses shall every word be established." Jesus had several witnesses. The Bible had 54 of the best scholars to make sure the translation was right.

Also, every verse can be confirmed by a different verse somewhere in Old or New Testament. **Spiritual things are confirmed by spiritual things. If you don't have spiritual discernment, then your opinion doesn't matter.** The spirit created our existence, and outside the view point of God, you're in a delusion.

**2 Peter 1:20** says, "Knowing this first that no prophecy of the scripture is of any private interpretation." Mahammad had a private interpretation of what that spirit was telling him, and everyone had to take his word for it. Prophets of the Bible received prophecy that corresponded with the other prophet's prophecy that actually came true, which gives validity to the prophet and the prophecy itself. One spirit working in different individuals. Mahammad's revelations came from a spirit not of God, because every time he received a revelation he was terrified, and God has not given us a spirit of fear. I can bear witness, because I have experienced both evil and the Holy Spirit. I have spiritual discernment, so I can say what I say with confidence. Until you experience the Holy Spirit, you'll never understand. The Holy Spirit makes you humble, and fills you with love. The sun represents the one true God that gives light and life to everything. The moon and the stars represent Lucifer and his fallen angels. The moon gets its light from the sun. **The devil only has as much power as God allows him to have.** Sometimes the moon and stars can be interpreted as light, but it takes darkness to see them in the first place. And no marvel; for Satan himself is transformed into an angel of light. In the bible, angels are referred to as stars.

Water gives life to all living things on the earth. God gives life to all living things on the earth. People would rather drink anything else but water. People chase after everything else but God. When water is polluted it's not water any more. When people pollute God's word into whatever interpretation they feel comfortable with, it's not God's word anymore.

**John 1:1 says, "In the beginning was the Word, and the Word was with God, and the Word was God."**

**1 Peter 1:25 says, "But the word of the Lord endureth for ever. And this is the word which by the gospel is preached unto you."**

**Galatians 1:9 says, "As we said before, so say I now again, If any man preach any other gospel unto you than that ye have received, let him be accursed."**

# WORDS ARE SPIRIT AND WITCHCRAFT IS EVERYWHERE

**(We can put spirits in motion with our words. Words are spirit.)**

**Proverbs 25:28 says, "He that hath no rule over his own spirit is like a city that is broken down, and without walls."**

Read **Leviticus 19:31 - 20:6 - 20:27...Deuteronomy 18:10 & 11... 1 Samuel 28... 2 Kings 21:6... 2 Kings 23:24... 1 Chronicles 10:13... 2 Chronicles 33:6... Isaiah 8:19... Isaiah 19:3... Micah 5:12... Nahum 3:4... and Galatians 5:20**. It is a vile abomination to practice witchcraft and sorcery. Wigi boards, voodoo, doing satanic rituals, doing enchantments, and praying to the dead is witchcraft and sorcery. Channeling the spirit of your ancestors is sorcery.

Leviticus 19:31 KJV "Regard not them that have familiar spirits, neither seek after wizards, to be defiled by them: I am the LORD your God."

Leviticus 20:6 KJV "And the soul that turneth after such as have familiar spirits, and after wizards, to go a whoring after them, I will even set my face against that soul, and will cut him off from among his people."

Leviticus 20:27 KJV "A man also or woman that hath a familiar spirit, or that is a wizard, shall surely be put to death: they shall stone them with stones: their blood shall be upon them."

Deuteronomy 18:10-14 KJV "There shall not be found among you any one that maketh his son or his daughter to pass through the fire, or that useth divination, or an observer of times, or an enchanter, or a witch, Or a charmer, or a consulter with familiar spirits, or a wizard, or a necromancer. For all that do these things are an abomination unto the LORD: and because of these abominations the LORD thy God doth drive them out from before thee. Thou shalt be perfect with the LORD thy God. For these nations, which thou shalt possess, hearkened unto observers of times, and unto diviners: but as for thee, the LORD thy God hath not suffered thee so to do."

**The reason God brought all the plagues onto Egypt when Pharaoh wouldn't release the Israelites, was to show the Israelites that God's power is way more advanced than the witchcraft demonic power the Egyptians had.** God wanted to convince the Israelites, so they would believe and always have faith in the one true God. God wanted to show them they didn't need any spirit but his.

**Witchcraft is everywhere**, words are witchcraft, if you don't have anything good to say, dont say anything at all. Speaking negative and vain words in the atmosphere will give spirits ammunition to act on. We can put spirits in motion with our words. Words are spirit. **Proverbs 17:27** says, "He that hath knowledge spareth his words: and a man of understanding is of an excellent spirit." **Proverbs 18:21** says, "Death and life are in the power of the tongue: and they that love it shall eat the fruit thereof." **Matthew 12:37** says, "For by thy words thou shalt be justified, and by thy words thou shalt be condemned."

**Portals and energy fields open up when demonic rituals and blood sacrifices occur.** The more people participate in wickedness, the more evil spirits are released into our dimension. The plan is to fill the world up with sin, so that when the advanced demons are released, they will have a multitude of people to possess and destroy. Demonic possession is all over the place. **The zombie apocalypse is not only about half dead starving homeless people. It's about wild, out of control, demon possessed people.**

Witchcraft in America involve Hollywood, music industry, secret societies, and even pharmaceuticals. Anything that is set up to appear efficient, but is actually incompetent, is witchcraft and trickery. **There is a practice in voodoo called shifting where you can shift a sickness to one part of the body to the other, but without power to actually heal. This form of witchcraft keeps you coming back, in a cycle, to profit the witchdoctor. That's what pharmaceutical medicine does. It helps the symptoms in one area but gives you a host of problems somewhere else to keep you buying one medication after the other.** God created the Herbs as our natural medicine but we go to the middle man and get a genetically modified version in the form of pharmaceuticals.

**Jeremiah 6:16** says "Thus saith the Lord, Stand ye in the ways, and see, and ask for the old paths, where is the good way, and walk therein, and ye shall find rest for your souls. But they said, We will not walk therein."

# GOD MADE DRUGS ON EARTH AS THEY ARE IN HEAVEN

Frankincense and Myrrh are classified as drugs in Enoch 28. Drugs is medicine, and all herbs are medicine allong with fruit. Water is medicine. Everything god wants us to put in our bodies is medicine. Everything we eat results in certain endorphines released in our brain. A tired depressed person can drink a glass of water with a teaspoon of pepper to feel better and get motivated. Although the person's mine was altered from tired to allert, we classify drugs according to its ability to stimulate the pineal gland. When the pineal gland is stimulated, a person becomes relaxed, sedated and connected to the spirit one has. Every food has a purpose in providing the body with what it needs.

**Enoch 28:2** says, **"There I beheld choice trees, particularly those which produce the sweet-smelling drugs, frankincense and myrrh; and trees unlike to each other."**

**Matthew 2:11** says, "And when they were come into the house, they saw the young child with Mary his mother, and fell down, and worshipped him: and when they had opened their treasures, they presented unto him gifts; gold, and **frankincense**, and myrrh."

**Song of Solomon 3:6** says, "Who is this that cometh out of the wilderness like pillars of smoke, perfumed with **myrrh** and **frankincense**, with all powders of the merchant?"

**Song of Solomon 4:6** says, "Until the day break, and the shadows flee away, I will get me to the **mountain of myrrh**, and to the **hill of frankincense**."

**Leviticus 2:16** says, "And the priest shall burn the memorial of it, part of the beaten corn thereof, and part of the oil thereof, with all the **frankincense** thereof: it is an offering made by fire unto the LORD."

**Leviticus 2:2** says, "And he shall bring it to Aaron's sons the priests: and he shall take thereout his handful of the flour thereof, and of the oil thereof, with all the **frankincense** thereof; and the priest shall burn the memorial of it upon the altar, to be an offering made by fire, of a sweet savour unto the LORD:"

**Nehemiah 13:5** says, "And he had prepared for him a great chamber, where aforetime they laid the meat offerings, the **frankincense**, and the vessels, and the tithes of the corn, the new wine, and the oil, which was commanded to be given to the Levites, and the singers, and the porters; and the offerings of the priests."

**Exodus 30:8** says, "And when Aaron lighteth the lamps at even, he shall burn incense upon it, **a perpetual incense before the LORD throughout your generations. (Cannabis hemp is the incense that has lasted throughout the generations)**

**Revelation 18:13** says, "And cinnamon, and odours, and ointments, and frankincense, and wine, and oil, and fine flour, and wheat, and beasts, and sheep, and horses, and chariots, and slaves, and souls of men."

**Ecclesiastes 3:1** says, **"To everything there is a season, and a time to every purpose under the heaven." (On earth as it is in heaven)**

**Enoch 31:2-5** says, "...and arrived at the garden of righteousness. In this garden I beheld, among other trees, some which were numerous and large, and which flourished there. 3. Their fragrance was agreeable and powerful, and their appearance both varied and elegant The tree of knowledge also was there, of which if any one eats, he becomes endowed with great wisdom. 4. It was like a species of the tamarind tree, bearing fruit which resemnled grapes extreemely fine; and its fragrance extended to a considerable distance I exclaimed, How beautiful is this tree, and how delightful is its appearance! 5. Then holy Raphael, an angel who was with me, answered and said, This is the tree of knowledge, of which thy ancient father and thy aged mother ate, who were before thee; and who obtaining knowledge, their eyes being opened, and knowing themselves to be naked, were expelled from the garden.

**Deuteronomy 32:28** says, "For they are a nation void of counsel, neither is there any understanding in them."

**1 Kings 4:29** says, "And God gave Solomon wisdom and understanding exceeding much, and largeness of heart, even as the sand that is on the sea shore."

**Job 15:9** says, "What knowest thou, that we know not? What understandest thou, which is not in us?"

**Job 17:4** says, "For thou hast hid their heart from understanding: therefore shalt thou not exalt them."

**Job 20:3** says, "I have heard the check of my reproach, and the spirit of my understanding causeth me to answer."

**Job 28:12** says, "But where shall wisdom be found? And where is the place of understanding?"

**Job 32:8** says, "But there is a spirit in man: and the inspiration of the Almighty giveth them understanding."

**Proverbs 24:7 says, "Wisdom is too high for a fool: he openeth not his mouth in the gate."**

**The herbs and fruit are God's natural medicine**. There are hundreds of thousands of herbs and fruit that people have never heard of. We are more familiar with herbs such as mint, dandelion, ginseng, ginger, turmeric, cinnamon, and pepper is actually fruit. **The herbs kill parasites, keep the body cleaned out, and give us everything we need to be healthy. All herbs and fruit have vitamin c. I believe vitamin c is vitamin Christ, which is what and who we need the most of.**

**Revelation 21:4** says, "And God shall wipe away all tears from their eyes; and there shall be no more death, neither sorrow, nor crying, neither shall there be any more pain: for the former things are passed away." **Cannabis, the poppy plant, and coca leaves help take away death, sorrow, and pain. These are three herbs that God gave man which have heavenly effects. The Devil knows this and has created a way to make them have negative effects.** The poppy plant eliminates pain, has sedative properties, and the seeds have anti-cancer properties. The coca leaves is a stimulant with antioxidants, vitamins and minerals that helps eradicate sickness. Cannabis makes you happy, peaceful, stimulates the pineal gland with a meditative effect, and when ingested eradicates pain and disease. Sleep and water helps the body heal, so cannabis happens to make you thirsty and get plenty of rest. Cannabis ranks as the most medicinal herb on the planet.

**Psalm 104:14** says, "He causes the grass to grow for the cattle and **herb for the service of man**: that he may bring forth food out of the earth."

**Genesis 1:29-31** says, "And God said, Behold, I have given you every herb bearing seed, which is upon the face of all the earth, and every tree, in the which is the fruit of a tree yielding seed; to you it shall be for meat. And to every beast of the earth, and to every fowl of the air, and to everything that creepeth upon the earth, wherein there is life, I have given every green herb for meat: and it was so. And God saw everything that he had made, and, behold, it was very good. And the evening and the morning were the sixth day."

Since God said that everything he created was very good, then we don't have dominion to say it isn't. God didn't say every herb except for Cannabis. He said every herb. Our responsibility is to find out the purpose for what God created instead of passing judgment on it. Anything can be bad when you use it outside of its season, time, and/or purpose. God said to eat. Not to snort, or inject into the veins. Smoking is burning incense, but smoking as we know it today is more indulging because it is illegal, which makes it expensive and over priced. Gluttony is eating too much, so cannabis is an herb for food that we should eat according to its service and not engage in gluttony. There is no hole in our body for a needle to go. Leave fast food alone, for it is processed according to Satan's devices. Not I, but God said every green herb that yeild seed was very good.

Cannabis hemp is a solution for Cancer, Muscular Dystrophy, HIV/AIDS, Glaucoma, Hypertension, Fatigue, Asthma, ALS, Osteoporosis, Spasticity, Parkinson's, Alzheimer's, Multiple Sclerosis, Seizures, Epilepsy, Tourette's, Depression, PTSD, OCD, Bipolar, Stress,

ADD/ADHD, Anxiety, Crohn's, Diabetes, Nausea, Gastrointestinal Disorders, Cachexia, Anorexia, Appetite Loss, Inflammation, Arthritis, Pain, Insomnia, Fibromyalgia, Spinal Injury, Phantom Limb, Migraine/Headaches, Cramps, and Sleep Apnea.

Cannabis is oil is the quickest way to get the health benefits of healing from major conditions is to extract all the medicine from the buds with grain alcohol, burn off the alcohol to leave pure oil that can cure anything depending on the strand. There are many different strands but the highly sedative Indicia strand is more potent than the Sativa. To make and ingest cannabis oil would leave a disease free society.

Cannabis stimulates the pineal gland to produce melatonin. Melatonin is what keeps every cell in our body healthy. People with high melatonin stay cancer free, and people with low melatonin can easily catch cancer. THC attaches to cancer cells and kills them. Cannabis hemp (Marijuana) doesn't kill brain cells. The lack of oxygen kills brain cells. Short term memory loss only occurs through abuse and the lack of oxygen to the brain. Research has found that smoking cannabis does not hurt the lungs. Tobacco can cause lung cancer and oxygen deficiency when it is sprayed with chemicals and wrapped in poisonous paper. Tobacco is for absorbing venum and toxins when used topically, and its effective when ingested as an herb that helps the body with various ailments. We all have nicotine receptors in our brain. Why would God created us with a receptor for something we shouldn't recieve.

When cannabis is smoked, some of the healing properties are burned off. Smoke is not the designated way for man to take in nutrients. However, inhaling the smoke provides mental benefits that are highly therapeutic by stimulating the pineal gland. When cannabis is ingested, all of the healing properties can be used by the body. If we used cannabis like we use salt and pepper, we would be extremely healthy.

To forget is a characteristic of meditation. Cannabis helps one to momentarily forget trauma and/or stress to focus on what's important to the soul. Cannabis makes you aware of your spirit and spirits that are around you. It actually activates the pineal gland, which is the way spirits connect with people. This is why people get paranoid when the THC attaches to the receptors in their brain. They become aware of spirits in them, as well as spirits that are around them. It helps one become aware of good and evil. This is why I believe its the tree of knowledge of good and evil. We have endocannabinoid receptors in our brain to receive cannabis. There are many cannabinoids in cannabis, and they vary according to the strand. God wouldn't have created us with the receptors if we weren't supposed to receive it. Every doctor knows that drinking lots of water and rest is essential to healing. If people got 'the munchies' and only ate healthy, just immagine how productive our society would be. Junk food defiles the mind and soul, therefore we have been coerced into going against our own interest. Cannabis makes you thirsty and get plenty of rest. It is the medication of all medications that's profoundly misunderstood.

The hemp plant was one of mankind's first cultivated plants and there is quite a lot to educate oneself about this great historical plant. With the help of the hemp plant we, as a society could eliminate smog from current fuels, create a cleaner energy source that can replace nuclear power, remove radioactive waste from the soil, and eliminate smog from our skies in more industrialized areas. The hemp plant could assist in eliminating non-biodegradable plastics and cars by reintroducing Henry Ford's 100 year old dream of building cars made from hemp with a plastic hemp car body that can withstand a blow 10 times as great as steel without denting. It weighs 1 thousand pounds less than steel, so it can improve gas mileage. Cannabis can run on a vegetable oil based all natural hemp fuel, and has a completely biodegradable body. Nationwide hemp production could eliminate deforestation by converting current paper to hemp paper which can be recycled up to 8 times instead of using wood pulp which is only recyclable up to 3 times. Also we could thrive from eating hemp seeds and feeding it to our animals and livestock.

Industrial hemp can make our future roads, highways, and freeways from hemp based concrete that lasts for centuries. We can benefit from the hemp plant's attributes such as oxygen production. Cannabis hemp has a dense root structure that puts nutrients and nitrogen back in the soil. Chemicals in cannabis can be used in medicines and are estimated to treat around 250 diseases and illnesses. Finally, we could make an estimated 50,000 products ranging from building composites, cellophane, dynamite, shampoo, textiles, twine and yarn. If the US grew industrial hemp it could stop wars, save the environment, boost our economy, improve general health and well-being, end our reliance on any foreign entity, and save mankind from itself.

I believe that the demonization of cannabis hemp is one of the greatest example of deception known to man. The 'Law of the Land' is that every God given resource from the earth is for the service of man, and if you don't work you don't eat. The Law of Water says that you can't partake of the God given resources unless you have enough water (money) current (currency) to put in a river (bank), so you have to maintain water (cash) flow that's guided by the (river) bank. To freely take part in the resources of the earth is called freedom, thus the law, 'Freedom of Religion'. If the church would have come together with the knowledge that Cannabis is an herb, and God said that it's good, millions of lives would have been saved from disease and unnecessary criminal charges. Evil prevails when God's people do nothing, and the children of God are destroyed for the lack of knowledge. It's amazing how people can go against their own interest with religious zeal. We have opposed our own health, sustainability, peace, an unlimited reproducing resource, and a pollution and nuclear energy free world by opposing cannabis hemp.

****Despite Industrial Hemp having 50,000 known uses, Dupont, Rockefeller, Hearst, Mellon, and their constituents infiltrated the industrial and medicinal market with political propaganda. Dupont created Nylon, owned General Motors, and was one of the top ten U.S. based petroleum and natural gas producers and refiners. Rockefeller owned Standard Oil and was soon known as the richest man in modern history. They knew that if people realized the resource that Cannabis Hemp was, they would lose their power. Monopolies put vast amounts of power in the hands of a few people. Monopolies and capitalism is why we are in the trouble we're in now. There would be no monopolies, or capitalism if Cannabis Hemp was used to its capacity. Medical marijuana has no seeds, because the powers that be want to control all the seeds in order to have a monopoly like they have on everything else. The seeds have amazing health benefits. When the high concentrated cannabis oil is ingested at a particular rate, based on the CBD's in the particular strand, it is a cure for almost anything. Cannabis is supposed to have seeds. THC is not the only important compound in cannabis. Seedless cannabis occurs by depriving the female plant from pollenating, which results in higher THC levels. Endocannabinoids are compounds in cannabis that cure disease without the intense euphoria. They knew cannabis was a cure all in the 1800's, but this knowledge would make the medical, oil and textile industry obsolete. The modern day Knights Templar own Pharma.

Cannabis also brings people together in peace, and the powers that be didn't want black and white people coming together in peace. They wanted to continue the divide and conquer strategy. Around the 1930's, they changed the name from Cannabis to Marijuana in order to demonize it. One public interest story they used to get white Americans to accept illegalization of Marijuana was this: "It made white girls desire black men and Mexicans, and made black men look white men in the eyes." Most people remember the promotion of the idea that black men on marijuana makes a 'crazed Negro.' Anytime, they want to pass a law, they pull the race card and ignorant, insecure racist fall for it every time.

Wall Street needed slaves and people buying a bunch of stuff they don't need. Cannabis helps people content with the simple things in life, and Wall Street wouldn't get rich with people content with the simple things in life. Cannabis is a deprogramming herb that keeps one in a state of meditation. It's hard to brainwash a person in a meditative state. It's hard to enslave a person in a meditative state. Wall Street need us to over consume and fix our homes up like MTV cribs. America consumes more than any nation in the world, but we're not even self-sustainable. We forgot that this country was built on the backs of slaves. We forgot that food and everything we need comes from the earth freely. We were brainwashed into believing that we were in a free country. We thought that electing a black president would change things. We thought that cannabis hemp was bad. We are addicted to lies more than anything.

When a minister of God's word says that Cannabis or Marijuana is bad. They are ignorantly calling God a lie. God said in Genesis 1:29 & 30 that all fruit and green herb that yield seed is for meat. Cannabis is a green herb that yield seed. And God said it was very good. The bud of Cannabis is a fruit and herb at the same time. The bud is the fruit of the plant, and the entire plant has over 50,000 uses. Everything God created is good for something and cannabis hemp is good for everything on earth. Putting the creation before God and using it out of its season, time, and purpose is bad.

Romans 3:4 says "Let God be true, but every man a liar; as it is written, that thou might be justified in thy sayings, and might overcome when thou art judged." The soul depends on the true word of God. Get knowledge, wisdom is the principle thing, and in all thy getting, get understanding.

. Read Genesis 1:11, v12, v29, v30, chapter 2:5, 3:18, 9:3, Deuteronomy 11:10, Job 38:27, Psalm 104:14, Proverbs 15:17, Isaiah 66:14, Romans 14:2, Hebrews 6:7, Isaiah 18:4, 26:19, 37:27, 42:15, and Leviticus 16:12 says, "And he shall take a censer full of burning coals of fire from off the altar before the Lord, and his hands full of sweet incense beaten small (meaning broken down), and bring it within the vail." Exodus 30:8 says, "And when Aaron lighteth the lamps at even, he shall burn incense upon it, a perpetual incense before the Lord throughout your generations."

Perpetual (definition):

(usually prenominal) eternal; permanent

2. (usually prenominal) seemingly ceaseless because often repeated: your perpetual complaints

3. (horticulture) blooming throughout the growing season or year

noun

4. (of a crop plant) continually producing edible parts: perpetual spinach

5. a plant that blooms throughout the growing season

* Cannabis has been here since the beginning and has lasted throughout all generations.*

**1 Kings 3:3 says** "And Solomon loved the Lord, walking in the statutes of David his father: only he sacrificed and burnt incense in high places**.**"

I advise you to read **2 Chronicles 26:16-23**. King Uzziah had pride and thought he could burn incense at the alter of incense, but it was designated for the priest. He had pride in his heart and resisted correction, so God smote him with leprosy. Why would Uzziah fight against the ordainance of God for a smell. It had to be something more significant about the incense for him to resist correction.

**2 Corinthians 11:23 says,** "Are they ministers of Christ? (I speak as a fool) I am more; in labours more abundant, in stripes above measure, in prisons more frequent, in deaths often." **Paul was saying that he suffered more than anyone, and labored more than anyone else in the ministry. However, he said, "I speak as a fool", because he was wise enough to know that what God did for him he could do for someone else. I'm saying**

**that I have confidence in my discernment, but not enough to claim what the incense was without being sure. I just can't see it being anything else but the greatest herb in the world, and all herbs can be burned as incense.**

The priest in the Old Testament burned incense unto God. It doesn't say what type of incense, and I'm not saying it was Cannabis. However, cannabis is a sweet smelling incense. It has a good smell and it helps with spiritual connection by stimulating the pineal gland. If you have the Holy Spirit, you connect with the Holy Spirit. If you have a foul spirit, you connect with a foul spirit. Whatever is in you will come out. Cannabis smells like a pine cone, and the pineal gland is so called because it's shaped like a pine cone. It has a characteristic of meditation. That's why people relax and chill out. To momentarily forget is a characteristic of meditation. Some things are necessary to forget. Military soldiers need to forget death and destruction and become one with their heart. Demons always look to control a person's mind after traumatic and crisis situations, because that's when people are most vulnerable. Everything about the sacrifices the priest were to make dealt with preparation. The incense was for mental preparation before going into the holy of holies. They needed a self evaluation before comming into the presence of God because their life was on the line. Cannabis actually makes one sober.

The definition of sober is:

1. not intoxicated or drunk. (There is no compound in cannabis that is toxic)

2. habitually temperate, especially in the use of liquor.

3. quiet or sedate in demeanor, as persons. (Cannabis makes people quiet, and causes sedating demeanors)

4. marked by seriousness, gravity, solemnity, etc., as of demeanor, speech, etc.:

5. subdued in tone, as color; not gay or showy, as clothes. Modest

6. free from excess, extravagance, or exaggeration: sober facts. (Cannabis compels people to speak less and say what they mean.)

7. showing self-control: restraint. (Cannabis raises inhibitions to refrain from dangerous and violent activities)

**The Coca leaf is highly nutritious.** For instance, 100 grams of coca leaf supplies more than the US recommended daily intake of calcium, phosphorus, iron, and vitamins A, B2, and E. **Some doctors believe coca and other psychoactive plants may play a role in helping the brain function properly, particularly when used during times of poor nutrition and in stressful environments.** According to a study published by Harvard University in 1975 (Duke, J., D. Aulik and T. Plowman, Nutritional Value of Coca), **chewing 100 grams of coca is enough to satisfy the nutritional needs of an adult for 24 hours. Thanks to the calcium, proteins, vitamins A and E, and other nutrients it contains, the plant offers even better possibilities to human nutrition than the medicine that is commonly used today.**

**Traditional medical uses of coca are foremost as a stimulant to overcome fatigue, hunger, and thirst. It is**

**highly effective against altitude sickness. It also is used as an anesthetic for such ailments as headache, rheumatism, wounds and sores, etc.** Before stronger anesthetics were available, it was even used for broken bones, and childbirth. Because cocaine constricts blood vessels, the action of coca also serves to oppose bleeding, and coca seeds were used for nosebleeds. Indigenous use of coca has also been reported as a treatment for malaria, ulcers, asthma, to improve digestion, to regulate the bowels, as an aphrodisiac, and credited with improving longevity. Coca also dries the respiratory tract, aids scarring, anti-fermenting, anesthetic, analgesic, stimulant, analgesic, powerful anesthetic, prevents caries, affects Ca/P, metabolizes sugars, cardiac tonic, effective against altitude sickness, stimulates the salivary glands, equivalent to B12, increases hemoglobin, aids scarring, digestive, absorbent, anti-diarrhea, increases cerebral circulation, and reduces arterial hypertension.

Modern studies have shown many of these medical applications to be effective. 100 grams of coca leaf contains: Vitamin A: UI 14,000; Alpha carotene: 2.65mg; B1 (thiamine): 0.68mg; B6 (pyridoxine): 0.58mg; Beta carotene: 20mg; C (ascorbic acid): 53mg; H (biotin): 0.54mg; Nicotinic acid: 5mg. Also contains the trace elements: Aluminum: 49mg; Barium: 17mg; Boron: 24mg; Calcium: 1540mg; Copper: 1.1mg; Chromium: 0.23mg; Strontium: 204mg; Iron: 45.8mg; Phosphate: 911.8mg; Magnesium: 0.37mg; Manganese: 0.5mg; Potassium: 1.9mg; Sodium: 1110mg; and Zinc: 3.8mg.

**South Americans depend a lot on coca for their survival and nutrition. The powers that be spray poison over their crops. That results in destruction of the land, and extreme poverty for the people.**

**Poppy is for pain. The seeds are highly nutritious and less allergenic than many other seeds and nuts. Poppy seeds can be a source for anti-cancer drugs.** Nutritional value per 100 g (3.5 oz): Energy 2,196 kJ (525 kcal), Carbohydrates 28.13 g, Dietary fiber 19.5 g, Fat 41.56 g, Saturated 4.517 g, Monounsaturated 5.982 g, Polyunsaturated 28.569 g, Protein 21.22 g, Vitamins Vitamin A equiv. beta-carotene, Thiamine (B1) (74%) 0.854 mg, Riboflavin (B2) (8%) 0.100 mg, Niacin (B3) (6%) 0.896 mg, Vitamin B6 (19%) 0.247 mg, Folate (B9) (21%) 82 μg, Choline (11%) 52.1 mg, Vitamin E (12%) 1.77 mg. Trace metals include: Calcium (144%) 1438 mg, Iron (75%) 9.76 mg, Magnesium (98%) 347 mg, Manganese (109%) 2.285 mg, Phosphorus (124%) 870 mg, Potassium (15%) 719 mg, Sodium (2%) 26 mg, Zinc (74%) 7.0 mg, and Water 5.95 g.

We all have opioid receptors, and endocannabinoid receptors in our brain. Endocannabinoid receptors, which we are born with to receive cannabis effects appetite, pain-sensation, mood, and memory. Opioid receptors are distributed widely in the brain, and are found in the spinal cord and digestive tract. Opiates are addictive because they connect with receptors 'delta OP1,' and 'mu OP3.' These rcceptors have physical dependence functions. Also connects with the Nociception receptor that has a development of tolerance function.

Addicts have been deprived of the truth, and the natural order of therapy. The Poppy plant, from which opiates derive, should be the first treatment for extreme pain but only short term. Then cannabis should be ingested until the pain goes away. Cannabis eradicates pain. The safest and effective way to get people off of drug addiction is by ingesting cannabis. Preferably cannabis oil. Ingesting cannabis oil is the supreme cure all. If everyone used cannabis oil, I'm convinced that sickness would be eradicated.

**Matthew 15:11** says, "Not that which goeth into the mouth defileth a man; but that which cometh out of the mouth, this defileth a man." **(The spirit of addiction and self – destruction is what defiles a man. Man is afflicted and vexed because of evil. If it wasn't for sin, we wouldn't have the need to medicate in the first place. Most diseases, especially mental disorders, have spirits attached to them, and Jesus is always the answer for healing.)**

The devil doesn't create anything. All he does is pervert what God created, and uses it to kill, steal and destroy. The Devil is the author of confusion. God loves us enough to give us what we need to be free from pain and the devil has used it to cause pain. Satan's main goal is to rule the world by deception. The globalist get their instructions directly from the Devil himself via rulers of the darkness and spiritual wickedness in high places. **What God made was in the book of life, and what the devil made was outside the book of life. The Devil specializes in corrupting the DNA of God's creation.**

**Proverbs 24:7** says, "Wisdom is too high for a fool: he openeth not his mouth in the gate."

**God's word says to guard your heart (pineal gland) because from the heart (pineal gland) are the issues of life. The problem is that many people don't guard their heart.** They let all kinds of crap in their heart by the pride and lusts of this world. Once all kinds of sin and abomination gets in the heart of a person, it has to come out one way or the other. The word says from the abundance of the heart the mouth speaks. That's why people get drunk and speak from the heart. If they have violence in their heart, they get violent. Whatever is in a man will come out. That's why they call alcohol spirits, because alcohol brings out the spirit and heart of a person. Whatever spirit that's in a man comes out when he drinks. This is the only reason, I feel, the Priest would burn incense (cannabis) unto God, on the altar of incense, because they had the right spirit and heart to do it.

**Jeremiah 17:9** says, "The heart is deceitful above all things, and desperately wicked: who can know it?

**Ecclesiastes 3:1** says, "To everything there is a season, and a time to every purpose under the heaven." Anything can be bad when you use it outside of its season, time, and/or purpose. . Herb is for the healing of the nations. Alcohol is to aid the herbs for a quicker healing process. Grain Alcohol can be used to extract the oils from herbs to make a more potent medicine. Vitamin E, some fruit, turmeric, and garlic thins the blood to help lower blood pressure. Grain alcohol thins the blood to help the herbs absorb into the blood easier, faster, and with a multiplied effect. Think of pouring syrup in milk. You have to stir the milk in order for the syrup to spread. When you poor syrup in water, it spreads faster without having to stir. Blood goes from milk to water when it's thinned by alcohol.

Alcohol helps one fall asleep when dealing with sickness and pain. Alcohol is only a seasonal antidote, and should be limited. Beer can be made from herbs and/or grain. Beer of today is made from rice, barely, and/or hops. Hops is an herb that has an abundant of health benefits. The darker the beer, the more barely or hops it contains. Most of the cheap beer now a days has harmful additives in it, as well as most flavorful liquor. Water is a daily antidote. Water can be used for health, or it can be used to drown. Drinking too much water can kill you. Every aspect of creation has to be dealt with according to knowledge, wisdom, and understanding. **Ecclesiastes 9:7** says, "Go thy way, eat thy bread with joy, and drink thy wine with a merry heart; for God now accepteth thy works." **Ecclesiastes 10:19** says, "A feast is made for laughter, and wine maketh merry: but money answereth all things." Then **Proverbs 20:1** says, "Wine is a mocker, strong drink is raging: and whosoever is deceived thereby is not wise." This is evidence that we have to be led by the Holy Spirit in all that we do. **Proverbs 16:2** says, **"All the ways of a man are clean in his own eyes; but the Lord weigheth the spirits."** Be led by the Holy Spirit, and when you get the Holy Spirit, you will know when you are making an idol out of something. We should always keep in mind to have no other gods before the almighty God.

**Job 28:28** says, "And unto man he said, Behold, the fear of the Lord, that is wisdom; **and to depart from evil is understanding.**"

**Proverbs 31:6** says, "Give strong drink unto him that is ready to perish, and wine unto those that be of heavy hearts." **John 14:27** says "Peace I leave with you, my peace I give unto you: not as the world giveth, give I unto you. Let not your heart be troubled, neither let it be afraid." Therefore, we are supposed to encourage ourselves in the comfort of the Holy Ghost. **God said let not your heart be troubled, so we shouldn't get to the point of needing to drink or smoke anything because of a heavy heart.** However, if one finds his/herself overwhelmingly stressed, **it's better to use what God created for stress, than to let stress shorten your life. Stress kills. However, when we are steadfast in faith through suffering, a good reward is always the outcome.**

**There are testimonies from people that God allowed to experience Heaven to come back and tell the people.** There is a river of life in Heaven that is alive and can flow right through your spiritual body. **One account says that when it flows through you, you experience extreme ecstasy and words can't explain the love, joy, peace, awareness, and the extreme energy felt. He said that via this river he was shown future events to warn people of what's coming.**

**Revelation 22:1-3** says, "And he shewed me a pure river of water of life, clear as crystal, proceeding out of the throne of God and of the Lamb. In the midst of the street of it, and on either side of the river, was there the tree of life, which bare twelve manner of fruits, and yielded her fruit every month: **and the leaves of the tree were for the healing of the nations.**" And there shall be no more curse: but the throne of God and of the Lamb shall be in it; and his servants shall serve him." **Cannabis is known as the herb for the healing of the nations, and the leaves on the Tree of Life are for the healing of the nations. That's just a correlation that cannot be ignored**.

If God gave us wonder foods to eradicate pain, sorrow, disease, which give us temporary peace, love, and happiness to deal with the hardships of life on earth; **you can only imagine what God has for us in Heaven. Revelation 2:7** says, "He that hath an ear, let him hear what the Spirit saith unto the churches; To him that overcometh will I give to eat of the tree of life, which is in the midst of the paradise of God." **It has to be some amazing fruit on the Tree of Life**. We haven't seen anything yet. **Don't worship the creation, only worship the creator, in which there is everlasting ecstasy.**

**Psalm 92:6** says, "A brutish man knoweth not; neither doth a fool understand this."

**The euphoria we get from sex is symbolism to the extreme euphoria we will have in Heaven.** I'm not saying we'll have sex in heaven, what I'm saying is that everything about God makes you feel good. If there are things that make you feel good on earth, everything will make you feel good in Heaven. Sex is an element of life and love. God is love, and God is life. **The natural things God created on earth that make us feel good, is only a shadow of things in heaven that will make us feel excellent.**

**Matthew 6:10** says, "Thy kingdom come, Thy will be done in earth, as it is in heaven."

**People are addicted to drugs because they chase a heavenly state of mind, but never find it without Jesus.** People want to escape the stress of the world, and the demons that attack the mind. This is why people who sell their soul to the devil stay high all the time. This is why people with mental disorders, which is mostly demon possession, stay drugged up all the time. Jesus can free us from any addiction, but we have to want it gone. **The Holy Spirit will comfort you from all stress and strain.** We have to encourage ourself in the Holy Spirit by singing, reading the Bible, and praying. Some spirits only come out by fasting and praying. Whatever we are led in the Spirit to do, will comfort us. **Bad habits are broken by gaining good habits.** Fill your day up with healthy activities, and you won't have time for the unhealthy ones. **Separation is always the key to overcoming strongholds, because our flesh is too weak to resist familiar spirits. People are temples of a spirit. Either Holy or Evil.** People want to rid pain, stress, and frustration. **Anything that has a powerful dopamine release in the brain makes the brain**

**want it all the time. Sex is addictive, because sex releases large amounts of dopamine in the brain.**

**Psalm 53:2** says, "God looked down from heaven upon the children of men, to see if there were any that did understand, that did seek God."

There is no high like heaven, so heaven is where you need to be. There you'll be high on real life, which is incorruptible. No more pain, sorrow, or sickness. Eternal happiness, love, joy, and peace in paradise where the music is beyond your imagination, and where praising God is an eternal celebration. There is always something to do and you'll never be bored. First you have to get delivered from the spirit of addiction. The spirit of addiction and self-destruction is what defiles the temple. Every self-destructive addiction has a spirit behind it, and foul spirits is what corrupts DNA and keeps us out of the Book of Life. Foul spirits are what defile the temple.

There are many people with diverse strongholds in the world. The Devil is the accuser of the brethren, and is trying to use sin (doors that we open up to evil spirits) to claim us for eternal damnation. We have the power to be free as long as we have the truth. Jesus is the way, truth, and life. God understands why people get high. He knows we don't have a clue of who we really are. He knows our flesh is weak, but God's strength is made perfect in our weakness. He's just shaking his head, because if we only knew what's waiting for us in heaven (Tree of Life), we wouldn't want a thing on earth. God wants us to love the creator over the creation. If you put anything before God, you are breaking the first Commandment: "Thou shalt have no other gods before me." He who has an ear, let him hear.

**"Thy kingdom come, thy will be done in earth, as it is in heaven."**

**Matthew 11:25** says, "At that time Jesus answered and said, I thank thee, O Father, Lord of heaven and earth, because thou hast hid these things from the wise and prudent, and hast revealed them unto babes."

**1 Corinthians 1:27** says, "But God hath chosen the foolish things of the world to confound the wise; and God hath chosen the weak things of the world to confound the things which are mighty."

**Isaiah 42:16** says, "And I will bring the blind by a way that they knew not; I will lead them in paths that they have not known: I will make darkness light before them, and crooked things straight. These things will I do unto them, and not forsake them."

**1 Peter 1:12-14** says, "Unto whom it was revealed, that not unto themselves, but unto us they did minister the things, which are now reported unto you by them that have preached the gospel unto you with the Holy Ghost sent down from heaven; which things the angels desire to look into."

**13.** Wherefore gird up the loins of your mind, be sober, and hope to the end for the grace that is to be brought unto you at the revelation of Jesus Christ;

**14.** As obedient children, not fashioning yourselves according to the former lusts in your ignorance:

**Romans 8:1** says, "There is therefore now no condemnation to them which are in Christ Jesus, who walk not after the flesh, but after the Spirit."

**Romans 8:28-31** says, "And we know that all things work together for good to them that love God, to them who are the called according to his purpose."

**29.** For whom he did foreknow, he also did predestinate to be conformed to the image of his Son, that he might be the firstborn among many brethren.

**30.** Moreover whom he did predestinate, them he also called: and whom he called, them he also justified: and whom he justified, them he also glorified.

**31.** What shall we then say to these things? If God be for us, who can be against us?

# CONCLUSION

**God is love. Jesus is God. Jesus is the truth. The truth will set you free from sin, and eternal bondage. Freedom is attained through Jesus. Freedom is in the mind.** Jesus is the way truth and the life, and no man cometh unto the Father but thru his son Jesus. Jesus had to give his life, so that he could send the Holy Ghost to us. The Holy Ghost is the comforter. The Holy Ghost will lead you to all truth. The Holy Ghost will help you endure till the end. Those who endure till the end will be saved. **Consider the caterpillar that endures till the end, then becomes a butterfly.**

**Pride is an abomination, so we have to give up our self-will, what we want to do, think, believe, and abide in truth.** If we have pride, we are acting like the Devil that was cast out of heaven. Why would God let anyone in Heaven that's going to be like the angels he kicked out? Humility is the key. How do you feel when your child is disobedient and constantly decides to do whatever he/she wants to do regardless of what you command? It's stressful huh? That's how we make God feel when we're disobedient without repentance, therefore God has to correct us through tough love to make us humble. When God corrects us when he is angry, it hurts like Haiti, Katrina, Sodom and Gomorrah. Sometimes we're not protected by God and the evils have open doors to come devour our lives. **The Devil operates through people, and that's why we have to abide in God and let God abide in us through the Spirit.**

**1John 4:4-7**

4 Ye are of God, little children, and have overcome them: because greater is he that is in you, than he that is in the world.

5 They are of the world: therefore speak they of the world, and the world heareth them.

6 We are of God: he that knoweth God heareth us; he that is not of God heareth not us. Hereby know we the spirit of truth, and the spirit of error.

7 Beloved, let us love one another: for love is of God; and every one that loveth is born of God, and knoweth God.

**A baby cries to his mother. The woman cries to her husband. All men cry out to God. God responds to a cry.** The son and the Father are 1, but no man cometh unto the Father unless he comes thru Jesus. **We have to cry out to Jesus. The Holy Ghost has to create in us a clean heart (pineal gland). We can't have a clean heart (pineal gland) with our own power. When God creates in us a clean heart, we have to guard our heart. From the heart (pineal gland) flows the issues of life.** From the abundance of the heart, the mouth speaks. You can discern what's in your heart by what you talk about. Jesus sends the Holy Ghost when we believe and the Holy Ghost is our comforter and protects our mind.

**Jesus told the disciples, "You believe because you have seen me, but blessed are those that believe and haven't seen. Just believe. Praising God keeps the Holy Ghost close. Sin pushes the Holy Ghost away. Many people think they believe, but don't have the Holy Ghost.** God has to help us believe, because the flesh only believes what it can see, so God has to reach out to us revealing his existence for us, to those according to his grace. I've had a few burning bush experiences, and like Moses, I also tried to make excuses why I couldn't do what God has called me to do. **I've been chosen to tell you the truth, because the truth will set you free. My father is a freedom fighter. I'm only here so we may not be slaves.** We are all slaves to sin until we are born again by the Holy Ghost. Our purpose is to serve the way Jesus came to serve. **Jesus said, "If you love me, feed my sheep**."

All people in the world of capitalism are slaves to the system. Be a servant to God, in which there is everlasting profit. The social system is evil because it's based on the love of money. The love of money is the root of all evil. What is meant for bad, God can turn it around for good. Jail is earthly symbolization of hell, and the electric chair symbolizes the lake of fire. Jail and hell separates us from life, freedom, love, and good food like the Tree of Life. Jail is modern day slavery. Slavery is correction. Who God loves he corrects. **Jesus is the truth, and the truth will set you free, spiritually and physically.**

**I love God, because he first loved me. We have to know how God has first loved us to really understand how much we should really love God**. Jesus answered my prayer, and has managed to keep me humble so that I can be with him and bear fruit, because God resist the proud. The Lord has taught me his promises and principles. **James 4:8** says, "Draw nigh to God, and he will draw nigh to you. Cleanse your hands, ye sinners; and purify your hearts, ye double minded." **2 Corinthians 10:5** says, "Casting down imaginations, and every high thing that exalteth itself against the knowledge of God, and bringing into captivity every thought to the obedience of Christ." **Matthew 10:39** says, "He that findeth his life shall lose it: and he that loseth his life for my sake shall find it." God wants a friend in us. God wants to walk with us, talk with us, and enjoy things with us.

**He already paid the price for our sins, he just wants to help us overcome. When you have the Lord, it's impossible to be alone.**

**Proverbs 16:3** says, "Commit thy works unto the Lord, and thy thoughts shall be established." No man is good, so we can't wait to be perfect before we decide to serve God. We have to commit our works to God and with Godly counsel our thoughts will be established. **God has called us to be examples of light. We can mess up our gifts and anointing by becoming influenced by people and their demons. 1 Peter 4:15** says, "But let none of you suffer as a murderer, or as a thief, or as an evildoer, or as a busybody in other men's matters." **Ecclesiastes 5:7** says, "For in the multitude of dreams and many words there are also divers vanities: but fear thou God." **Ecclesiastes 5:3** says, "For a dream cometh through the multitude of business; and a fool's voice is known by multitude of words."

God can work righteousness in us by the power of the Holy Ghost. **John 15:5** says, "I am the vine, ye are the branches: He that abideth in me, and I in him, the same bringeth forth much fruit: for without me you can do nothing." God made a way for us to bare good fruit and receive eternal life, and all we have to do is make a choice. Truth or the Lie, Life or Death, Freedom or Bondage, Love or Hate, Faith or Unbelief, Technology or Nature. Remember **1 Timothy 6:20**, which reads, "O Timothy, keep that which is committed to thy trust, avoiding profane and vain babblings, and oppositions of science falsely so called. **Key word is science.** Therefore, which some professing science have erred concerning the faith." In addition, Isaac Newton admitted that it had to be a God responsible for creation. He didn't believe the accuracy of the Genesis account, but he was coerced into making up a theory for the powers that be.. He just made the "Theory of Evolution" so the education system can brainwash the children. **The greatest trick the devil has pulled is convincing people he doesn't exist. That way he can convince people God doesn't exist, because God created the Devil.** God created us in his image and likeness, so we have intellect to think. **The Devil is mad because man has a chance for salvation, and he is doomed to the lake of fire. Don't be a fool for not using your brain that God created you with, and let the Devil take you to eternal separation from God**.

**Those who are led by the spirit of God can call themselves the sons of God. A denomination doesn't make you a son of God. The Holy Ghost makes you a son of God.** If you don't read the Bible you're taking God for granted. Every creation comes with a manual whether you like it or not. If you make a car, the manual will tell you what type of gas and oil to use. There are many ways I think life on Earth could be different, but that's like a child being ungrateful to his parents. Deal with it or get grounded for eternity. Our life on Earth is nothing to eternity. **Romans 8:18** says, "For I reckon that the sufferings of this present time are not worthy to be compared with the glory which shall be revealed in us. **1 Peter 3:17** says, **"For it is better, if the will of God be so, that ye suffer for well doing, than for evil doing."** Truth can hurt in the flesh. You haven't suffered until you sacrifice the flesh, which is mainly lust and pride. When you have the Holy Spirit, you love to receive the truth. That's why the word is that 2 Edge Sword, 2 sharp sides, Old and New Testament. **Hebrews 4:12** says, "**For the word of God is quick, and powerful, and sharper than any two edged sword, piercing even to the dividing asunder of soul and spirit, and of the joints and marrow, and is a discerner of the thoughts and intents of the heart.**"

Pastors, preachers, and teachers of Bible Christianity are only people. **Matthew 19:17 says, "And he said unto him, Why callest thou me good? there is none good but one, that is, God: but if thou wilt enter into life, keep the commandments." Jesus was good, but used every opportunity to teach. Jesus wasn't going to be on earth forever, so he wanted them to believe in what they couldn't see more than what they could see. Let God be true, and every man a liar**. You have to be called by God to preach. There are many preachers and pastors that weren't called, but they can quote Bible scripture. Those who are called have a job to lead people to Jesus through repentance. Baptism is symbolism of being born again, and when we get the Holy Ghost, which is the true baptism, we have to be led by the spirit of God in order to be a true child of God. If you don't read the Bible for yourself, you will lack discernment and won't be able to recognize the wiles of the Devil. Many people get the Holy Ghost but choose not to be led by the Holy Ghost. It's hard to hear the Holy Spirit when you're running your mouth. When we are not led by the Holy Spirit, we end up being led by another spirit. Other spirits result in demonic possession which defiles our DNA. Having defiled DNA takes a man out of the book of life.

Everyone has to be willing and make a decision to be led by the Holy Spirit in order to benefit from The Holy Spirit. The Kingdom of God is with the Holy Spirit. The Kingdom of Heaven is the House of God. The Kingdom of God can be in each one of us. We are called to be ambassadors of Christ. **2 Corinthians 5:20** says, "Now then we are ambassadors for Christ, as though God did beseech you by us: we pray you in Christ's stead, be ye reconciled to God." **Proverbs 13:17** says, "A wicked messenger falleth into mischief: but a faithful ambassador is health." **1 Peter 2:11** says **"Dearly beloved, I beseech you as strangers and**

**pilgrims, abstain from fleshly lusts, which war against the soul."**

**The Law of Attraction is God's law. As a man believeth in his heart, so is he. What you believe and meditate on is what you invoke. Meditate on the word of God. The Holy Spirit is close waiting for everyone to receive, for it's the comforter, friend, life guide, guard, and that still voice in your head that you have to train yourself to hear by praying in the name of Jesus and meditation**. Pray then listen for the spirit. TV has made people ADHD, making it hard for the mind to focus on one thing. That's why commercials are only so many seconds long, and there is innumerable programs and subliminal messaging to program your mind. Entertainment has made people desensitized to vanity. **Get the imagery out of your head and realize what you don't see is more real than what you do see. The Kingdom of God is at hand waiting for us to get the real picture.**

**Praising God is the norm in Heaven. Therefore get use to praising God on Earth. Praising God keeps us in touch with the Holy Spirit, and praising God pushes evil spirits away**. **Psalm 107:8-9** says, "Oh that men would praise the Lord for his goodness, and for his wonderful works to the children of men! For he satisfieth the longing soul, and filleth the hungry soul with goodness." This is why **Luke 12:10** says, "And whosoever shall speak a word against the Son of man, it shall be forgiven him; but unto him that blasphemeth against the Holy Ghost it shall not be forgiven." **The Holy Ghost is your connection, and your words can mess up your connection. 1 Corinthians 1:17** says, "For Christ sent me not to baptize, but to preach the gospel: not with wisdom of words, lest the cross of Christ should be made of none effect." Salvation is not gained through my wisdom, or any craftiness of man. **Salvation is**

**simply by the power in Jesus that keeps our DNA undefiled.**

**1 Corinthians 12:13** says, "**For by one Spirit are we all baptized into one body, whether we be Jews or Gentiles, whether we be bond or free; and have been all made to drink into one Spirit**." Everyone has a gift. God hasn't called everyone to do the exact same thing, but we all have to give God the glory in whatever we do and be led by the Holy Spirit. A house divided against itself cannot stand. **Many different members, but a part of the same body. Paul went to the Gentiles, and Peter stayed with the Jews. Same mission with different directions.** God's will is the will he has for each of our individual lives, which has an overall objective. We can't worry or covet other people within the body of Christ. **John 10:27** says, "My sheep hear my voice, and I know them, and they follow me." **There is only two colors for sheep, black and white**. **Life is about getting a clean heart, guarding the heart, and marriage to the Lamb of God**. Be transformed by the renewing of your mind, for we are the Bride of Christ. **1 Peter 2:9** says, "But ye are a chosen generation, a royal priesthood, a holy nation, a peculiar people; that ye should shew forth the praises of him who hath called you out of darkness into his marvelous light." **Matthew 12:37** says, **"For by thy words thou shalt be justified, and by thy words thou shalt be condemned." Ecclesiastes 12:13-14** says, **"Let us hear the conclusion of the whole matter: Fear God, and keep his commandments: for this is the whole duty of man. For God shall bring every work into judgment, with every secret thing, whether it be good, or whether it be evil."**

**Khary Ato - A Hebrew With Good News - Kingdom of God is at Hand like Finger Foods."**

Made in the USA
Columbia, SC
01 May 2025